TEXT BY
STEVE KEMP

PHOTOGRAPHS BY
KEN VOORHIS

GREAT SMOKY MOUNTAINS ASSOCIATION
Gatlinburg, Tennessee

EDITED BY: Dr. Edward Clebsch and Don Defoe
DESIGNED BY: Christina Watkins
ILLUSTRATED BY: Michael Taylor
COORDINATION AND TYPOGRAPHY BY: Steve Kemp
COVER PHOTOGRAPH BY: Adam Jones
PRINTED IN HONG KONG

13 14 15 16 17 18 19 20

ISBN 0-937207-09-8

Library of Congress Catalog Card Number: 93-91420

Great Smoky Mountains Association is a nonprofit organization which supports the educational, scientific, and historical programs of Great Smoky Mountains National Park. Our publications are an educational service intended to enhance the public's understanding and enjoyment of the national park. If you would like to know more about our publications, memberships, and projects, please contact: Great Smoky Mountains Association, P.O. Box 130, Gatlinburg, TN 37738 (865) 436-7318 www.SmokiesInformation.org.

For everyone who loves national parks
and strives to preserve them.

ACKNOWLEDGMENTS

If ever a book was a group effort, this was it. Dr. Ed Clebsch and Don DeFoe served as much more than editors, providing me with loads of invaluable information on the trees of the park from their over 50 years of combined work in the Smokies. National Park Service employees Glenn Cardwell, Keith Langdon, and Janet Rock enthusiastically and diligently contributed the fruits of their substantial field experience to this guide. Park librarian Annette Evans (whose name turns up in the acknowledgments of nearly every book published on the Smokies) was, as always, a huge help throughout this multi-year project. Lynne Davis and Jo Hoy saved the day several times over with their keen eyes as proofreaders.

Thanks to Dr. A.J. Sharp, Arthur Stupka, and the University of Tennessee Press for permission to adapt their tree and shrub key for use in this book. Thanks to Don Davis for his valuable information on logging. Thanks also to designer Christina Watkins who has singlehandedly done more to glorify literature on national parks than any other individual. And a special thanks to my boss, Terry Maddox, for allowing me the time to undertake this project and to Ken Voorhis and family for the six seasons they spent thrashing through hells, hollers, and highwaters shooting and reshooting the wonderful photographs for this book.

CONTENTS

INTRODUCTION

A WONDROUS DIVERSITY . . . .

Biological diversity is the hallmark of the Smokies, and this diversity is nowhere more evident than in the park's staggering variety of trees. Many superlatives have been conjured up over the years to express this diversity, including:

- "more species of native trees than in northern Europe"
- "more species of native trees than in any other North American national park."

In one unique demonstration, a college group on a field trip in the park reportedly appointed a student to throw a stone. The class marked the "stone's throw" distance and then counted the number of species of trees within it. They counted 30, about the same number of native species as in all of England, or over twice as many species as in 2.2 million acre Yellowstone National Park.

Exactly how many species of trees exist in the Smokies depends on your definition of tree. Like the difference between a stream and a river, there is a good deal of gray area in the mid-range. Further complicating the definition is the fact that many plants called shrubs in other areas reach tree-size proportions in the park. However, if we agree that a tree is a woody plant at least 10 feet tall and two inches in diameter with a well-defined stem and crown, then we can say that over 100 native species of trees occur in the Smokies, perhaps as many as 135.

Why such wondrous diversity? Mountains, glaciers, and weather are the big reasons. The Great Smoky Mountains provide a range of elevations from 875 to 6,643 feet. This altitudinal range mimics the latitudinal gamut you would experience driving north or south across the eastern United States, say from Georgia to Maine. Trees typical of the South, like umbrella magnolia and sweetgum, thrive in the lowlands of the Smokies while such northern species as mountain maple and American mountain-ash find suitable habitat at the higher elevations.

By their form, mountains also provide a variety of slopes and aspects. The habitat on a sunny, dry, south-facing ridge is very different from that on a cool, moist, northern slope, even if the two are at the same elevation.

Glaciers have affected diversity in the Smokies in that these mountains never had them. From 1.8 million to 10,000 years ago, glaciers scoured much of North America. They did not, however, quite reach as far south as the Smokies. Consequently, these mountains became a refuge for many species of plants and animals that were disrupted in their northern homes. The Smokies have, in fact, been relatively undisturbed by glaciers or ocean inundation for millions of years, allowing species here the luxury of time to evolve and diversify.

In terms of weather, the park's abundant rainfall and high summertime humidity provide excellent growing conditions for a wide variety of trees. Most trees, especially broadleaf species, require a goodly amount of water (Much of North America is tree-less where rainfall drops below 15 or 20 inches per year.) In the Smokies, the average annual rainfall varies from approximately 60 inches in the valleys to 88 inches on some peaks. During summer, the relative humidity in the park is about twice that of the Rocky Mountain region.

VIRGIN FORESTS . . . .

Not everyone agrees on exactly what constitutes a "virgin" forest. For one thing, most biologists prefer the term "old-growth." An old-growth forest, they maintain, contains the following attributes: a mix of young and old trees, many fallen and decaying logs, light gaps, trees in various stages of decline, a wide diversity of plant species, and no or only minimal past disturbance from logging or agriculture.

That established, biologists assert that ninety percent of the old-growth forest remaining in the eastern United States lies within the boundaries of Great Smoky Mountains National

Park. Working from logging records and field research, biologists estimate that there are about 125,000 acres (about 25 percent of the park) of old-growth in the Smokies.

Chances are you will recognize old-growth when you see it. Not all the trees are giants, but there will definitely be some large ones. Big tuliptrees, Eastern hemlocks, yellow buckeyes, yellow birches, Northern red oaks, or red spruces will often be the first species to catch your eye.

Another highly visible trait is openness. Though not always the case, many stands of old-growth have an unusual open or airy feel. You may have the sense that a person on horseback could pick their way through old-growth without too much difficulty. Dense thickets of shrub-sized plants common in disturbed forests may be scarce in old-growth.

Light gaps, created when one or more very large trees fall, are another old-growth characteristic. When a 150-foot tall tuliptree succumbs in a wind storm, it may bring down enough neighboring vegetation to open a ¼ acre hole in the forest canopy. The new window will allow many opportunistic species to get started, including tuliptrees, hemlocks, Fraser magnolias, and red maples.

A hike to an old-growth forest can be the highlight of a trip to the Smokies. However, there are few short and easy hikes to really spectacular old-growth areas. Inaccessibility was one prime reason that any forest in the Smoky Mountains went undisturbed. Yet for persons in reasonably good physical condition there are several areas reachable by a half-day's stroll. Listed here are some of the best hikes to old-growth forests.

◆ **Maddron Bald Trail** (Albright Grove)—Starts on a side road near Yogi's Jellystone Campground on highway 321, 15 miles east of Gatlinburg. It's seven miles roundtrip to go to, and around, Albright Grove.

◆ **Ramsey Cascade Trail**—Starts in the Greenbrier Cove area off highway 321 east of Gatlinburg. It's eight miles roundtrip to the waterfall.

◆ **Baxter Creek Trail**—Runs between the Big Creek area and Mt. Sterling in the northeast corner of the park. Take Exit 451 off Interstate 40 near the Tennessee/North Carolina border. The big trees start about 2.5 miles above the Big Creek trailhead. (It's 12.4 miles roundtrip if you go to the top of Mt. Sterling and take in the view from the fire tower.)

◆ **Laurel Falls Trail**—Starts from the Little River Road six miles west of Gatlinburg. It's two miles to the big trees; eight miles roundtrip if you go to the top of Cove Mountain.

◆ **Gregory Ridge Trail**—Starts from the Forge Creek Road which begins just past the Cable Mill area in Cades Cove. It's 11 miles roundtrip to Gregory Bald.

◆ **Fork Ridge Trail**—Starts from the Clingmans Dome Road. The first three miles descend through impressive spruce-fir and northern hardwood forests.

CHAMPION TREES . . . .

Since 1940, the American Forests organization has published its *National Register of Big Trees*. In this publication, the association lists the largest or "champions" of over 650 species of trees in the United States. Included in the list are the name of the finder, where the tree grows, and when it was last measured.

The association ranks its trees by circumference of the trunk at 4½ feet above the ground, total height, and average crown spread. For information on nominating a champion, contact: American Forests, P.O. Box 2000, Washington, DC 20013.

Great Smoky Mountains National Park has consistently been home to many national register champs. In 1946, the park could boast 23 champion trees. In 1961, the number was 22. By 1992, however, the total had fallen to seven. Many of the recent champions have been discovered by Will Blozan, an arborist in North Carolina and former forestry technician at Great Smoky

Mountains National Park.

Here are the 16 2004-05 champions and co-champions with their circumferences at breast height (4½ feet), their height, and average crown spread:

TREE	CBH	HT	ACS
Black cherry *Prunus serotina*	210"	134'	70'
Carolina silverbell *Halesia carolina*	152"	110'	43'
Cinnamon clethra* *Clethra acuminata*	10"	33'	12'
Cinnamon clethra* *Clethra acuminata*	9"	29'	10'
Devil's walking stick *Aralia spinosa*	23"	74'	16'
Eastern hemlock *Tsuga canadensis*	202"	165'	39'
Fraser magnolia* *Magnolia fraseri*	118"	121'	33'
Mountain laurel *Kalmia latifolia*	48"	25'	18'
Pin cherry *Prunus pensylvanica*	58"	75"	41"
Red hickory** *Carya glabra var. odorata*	154"	153'	79'
Red maple *Acer rubrum*	276"	141'	88'
Red spruce* *Picea rubens*	169"	123'	39'
Red spruce* *Picea rubens*	144"	146'	34'
Serviceberry *Amelanchier laevis*	78"	101'	36'
Striped maple *Acer pensylvanicum*	44"	77'	31'
Yellow buckeye*** *Aesculus octandra*	229"	136'	53'

Great Smoky Mountains National Park shelters more champion trees within its borders than any other national park or national forest in the East. In fact, the park's 16 champs represent one of the highest concentrations of record trees in the country. This distinction reflects the park's natural biological diversity, the integrity of its old-growth forests, and the success of preservation efforts by the National Park Service.

*co-champions. These trees are within 5 total points of the other co-champions of their species.

**The park's official checklist no longer recognizes the variety *odorata*. Most taxonomists would currently consider this tree a pignut hickory (*Carya glabra*). In general, the National Register of Big Trees tends to recognize many subspecies and varieties of trees that most taxonomists no longer regard as separate.
***Most taxonomists have changed the scientific name to *Aesculus flava*.

LOGGING DAYS . . . .

By the mid-1880s, trees were becoming big business in the Great Smoky Mountains. Although small scale, selective cutting was common before this time, the real logging boom occurred from approximately 1885-1939.

During the boom days, log-hauling steam locomotives whistled up many park drainages, including Little River, Hazel Creek, Middle Prong of the Little River (Tremont), Deep Creek, Big Creek, and others. Over 20 lumber companies and dozens of sawmills operated in the Smokies. Boom towns like Smokemont, Proctor, Tremont, and Elkmont, towns with as many as 1,200 residents, sprang up to house and provide services for the people who worked in the woods and the mills. These towns featured all the amenities, from movie theaters to schools and churches.

Clearcutting was the rule of the day and some companies cut from the river valleys all the way to the crest of State Line Ridge where the Appalachian Trail runs today. Black cherry, white ash, and tuliptree were the most sought after species, closely followed by American chestnut, white basswood, maples, oaks, yellow birch, silverbell, yellow buckeye, cucumber tree, and the pines. Red spruce was cut for papermaking and, during World War I, for airplane construction. Eastern hemlock was taken for the tannin in its bark (used for tanning hides) and for making paper. Wildfires often followed clearcutting, which further increased the erosion of soil from the steep mountain slopes.

How much timber was cut? Estimates vary, but conservative figures run close to two billion board feet, enough wood to build approximately 125,000 good-sized homes.

Just as the Great Smokies are home to a wondrous diversity of trees, they also host an amazing variety of tree diseases. During the 20th century, diseases permanently altered the composition of forests in the national park. During the 21st century, the changes may be even more profound.

By far the most damaging blights are those which have been inadvertently imported from other continents. Exotic insects, fungi, and other life forms, upon arriving in the New World, often find a seemingly limitless feast of trees. Even worse, the New World habitats usually lack the predators or plant defenses which controlled the species in its homeland. The result is an uncontrollable range expansion which may kill billions of trees.

Evidence of these intercontinental clashes are apparent in the absences they have left. A fungus from Asia became known as the "chestnut blight" when, between the years 1904 and 1940, it destroyed nearly every chestnut tree in the eastern United States.

If you had hiked in the Smokies a century ago, the chestnut would have been one of the most common trees that you encountered. Also one of the largest. A big chestnut had a circumference of 25 feet and towered 150 feet or more into the sky. They were the most dependable source of nuts of any tree in the Smoky Mountains, and bear, deer, birds, and humans benefitted greatly from their bounty.

Yet you can still see chestnuts in the Smokies. Trees whose trunks died 50 years ago still send up root sprouts which bear leaves and may grow to be 20 feet tall or so. Although most of these sprouts eventually die, perhaps someday natural selection will result in some blight resistant individuals surviving long enough to reproduce and pass on their resistance to offspring.

Some 95 percent of the large Fraser fir trees in the national park have been killed by a tiny European import called the balsam woolly adelgid. Although these aphid-like bugs co-exist fairly peaceably with their silver fir hosts in Europe, they annihilate their hosts here. Fraser fir trees exist only in the southern Appalachians and 75 percent live (or lived) in the park. The Fraser fir is also one of the key components of the unique spruce-fir forest which cloaks the highest peaks of the Smokies. As the forest continues to decline, there is the distinct possibility it will drag several species of insects and plants into extinction.

Small Fraser firs are still common in the park above 4,500 feet. Some even live long enough to bear cones. Perhaps this species will also survive long enough for resistant individuals to emerge.

While the effects of these non-natives may seem overwhelming today, many more exotics are on their way or have recently arrived. Here is a brief look at some of the major ones.

◆ **Hemlock woolly adelgid**—Similar to the balsam woolly adelgid which has devastated the park's Fraser firs, this tiny Asian insect now threatens the Smokies' magnificent Eastern hemlock trees. The insect is now widespread in the Smokies, though the National Park Service is using a number of effective treatment methods to save as many trees as possible. Several stands of old-growth hemlock are being treated, as are trees around picnic areas and campsites. Infected trees exhibit yellowing needles and may die within four years.

◆ **Dogwood anthracnose**—A non-native fungus (*Discula destructiva*) is now present throughout the park and has killed thousands of flowering dogwoods. Symptoms include purple-rimmed spots on the leaves, trunk sprouts, and cankers on the bark. Most trees die within three to five years of infection.

◆ **Gypsy moth**—This famous European nomad is approaching the park from the north, though biologists are now unsure if or when it will get here. If it does arrive, we can expect defoliation of up to 50,000 acres of hardwood forest per year with oaks (of which the Smokies harbor 11 species) suffering the brunt of the attack.

◆ **European mountain ash sawfly**—No one knows yet how harshly this insect will impact the Smokies' high elevation American mountain-ash trees. The insects already are defoliating many mountain ashes each year and a high rate of mountain ash mortality has been documented. Air pollution may be a contributing factor.

◆ **Butternut canker**—A non-native fungus appears to be killing some butternut (*Juglans cinera*) trees and reducing seed production in others. Throughout the southeastern United States, butternut populations are declining and the species is a candidate for protection under the Endangered Species Act. Butternuts are not common in the park.

◆ **Dutch elm disease**—This well-known European fungus killed several hundred American elms in the Little River watershed during the 1980s. Still, many populations in the park appear to remain healthy. The fungus can affect all three elm species in the Smokies: American, slippery, and winged.

◆ **Southern Pine Beetle**—Unlike the other tree-destroying organisms in this section, the Southern pine beetle is a native species and its predation on pines is considered a naturally occurring event in the national park. Mild winters appear to lead to heavy outbreaks of this insect. Beetle-killed stands of pine are easily identified by their orange needles.

TREE & SHRUB BLOOMING TIMES . . . .

Trees are marvelous conglomerations of shape, texture, color, and scent. And in their flowers, all four of these qualities can be experienced at once.

Fortunately for us, trees bloom during every month of the year in the Smokies. The following chart shows some of the best times to enjoy them.

SPECIES	WHEN BLOOMS	ELEVATION
Red maple	February-May	below 6,000'
Serviceberry	March to mid-May	below 6,000'
Redbud	late March to mid-April	below 2,000'
Flowering dogwood	mid- to late April	below 3,000'
Silverbell	mid-April to mid-May	below 5,000'
Flame azalea	late April to early July	below 6,000'
Mountain laurel	May through July	below 5,000'
Tuliptree	late April through May	below 5,000'
Fraser magnolia	April to June	below 5,000'
Pin cherry	April to June	above 3,000'
Catawba rhododendron	June	3,000-6,500'
Sourwood	Late June-July	below 5,000'
Rosebay rhododendron	June to July	below 5,000'
Witch-hazel	October-January	below 5,000'

FALL COLORS . . . .

Trees, celebrities at any time of year in the Smokies, become absolute *belles* of the ball in autumn. On sunny weekends in mid- or late October, some 60,000 people a day will make a pilgrimage to the park to see the "colors."

As a rule of thumb, the peak of fall colors will occur at some elevation in the Smokies between October 15 and November 10. At the higher elevations, where yellow birch, hobblebush, and red maple blaze against the evergreen backdrop, the peak usually occurs in early or mid-October. Be warned, however, that weekend traffic is extremely heavy in the park during peak color season, especially in Cades Cove and along the Newfound Gap Road. Visit during the week if you can, and if not, try some of the less crowded routes like the Blue Ridge Parkway, Balsam

Mountain Road, Foothills Parkway, Rich Mountain Road, and the Greenbrier Cove area.

USING THIS GUIDE . . . .

Our goal in producing this book has been to create a guide which allows people who are not professional botanists to identify trees in the Smokies during the "leaf on" season. Wherever we could, we avoided scientific terms. There were some compromises along the way, but we believe we've created a guide which non-scientists can use to successfully identify trees here. We did not include specific winter identification information on traits like leaf scars and bud scales because we felt that would make the book too large, complex, and expensive for our general audience.

There are, however, a couple of key terms which we do use that can be quickly learned and will go a long way in helping you identify trees.

The most important is the difference between a SIMPLE and COMPOUND leaf. Simple leaves are, in fact, simple: they are not divided into smaller leaflets. The majority of park trees and shrubs fall into this category, including maples, oaks, and elms.

Compound leaves are divided into several leaflets. You can tell a leaflet is not a simple leaf because its midrib is not woody and it does not have a bud at its base. Trees with compound leaves include hickories, walnuts, and sumacs.

OPPOSITE and ALTERNATE are the other key concepts. Opposite leaves grow directly opposite from one another on the twig. Alternate leaves are staggered along the twig. Most trees in the Smokies are alternate. One way to remember the opposite ones is with the acronym MAD buck. It stands for Maple-Ash-Dogwood and buckeye (yellow buckeye) and works as a rule of thumb.

When using this book, keep in mind the species are arranged by the following leaf types and in the following order:

- Simple leaves, not toothed along the edges *(pages 26-40)*
- Simple leaves, toothed *(pages 41-63)*
- Simple leaves, lobed *(pages 64-81)*
- Compound leaves *(pages 82-95)*
- Needle-like leaves *(pages 96-104)*

Identifying a tree often comes from looking at more than one characteristic. Leaves and bark are two of the best for trees in the Smokies, but sometimes habitat, twigs, buds, fruits, flowers, or other traits must be considered. Like solving most mysteries, identifying a tree often involves seeking out a number of clues.

One helpful piece of equipment for identifying trees is a pair of binoculars. On mature trees, the lowest leaves may be 40 or more feet above the ground. Binoculars will help you zoom in on the leaves and also see fruits, flowers, buds, and other important traits. A small magnifying glass or hand lens can be a big help when looking for hairs or other traits on leaves, buds, and twigs.

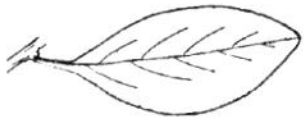

Simple Leaf

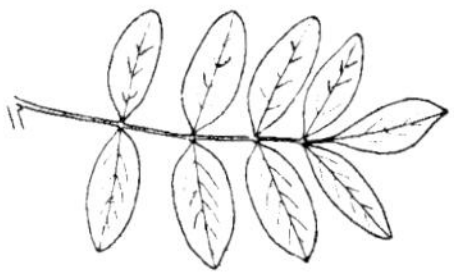

Compound Leaf (9 leaflets)

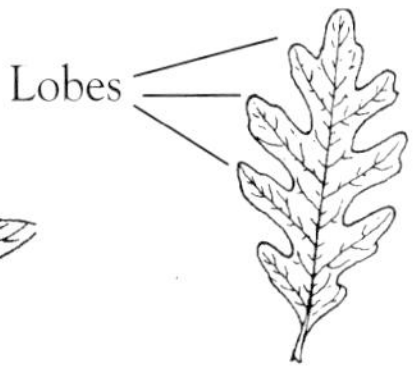

Lobes

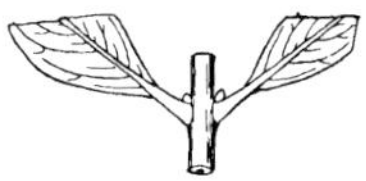

Opposite Leaves

Alternate Leaves

MAP OF GREAT SMOKY MOUNTAINS NATIONAL PARK

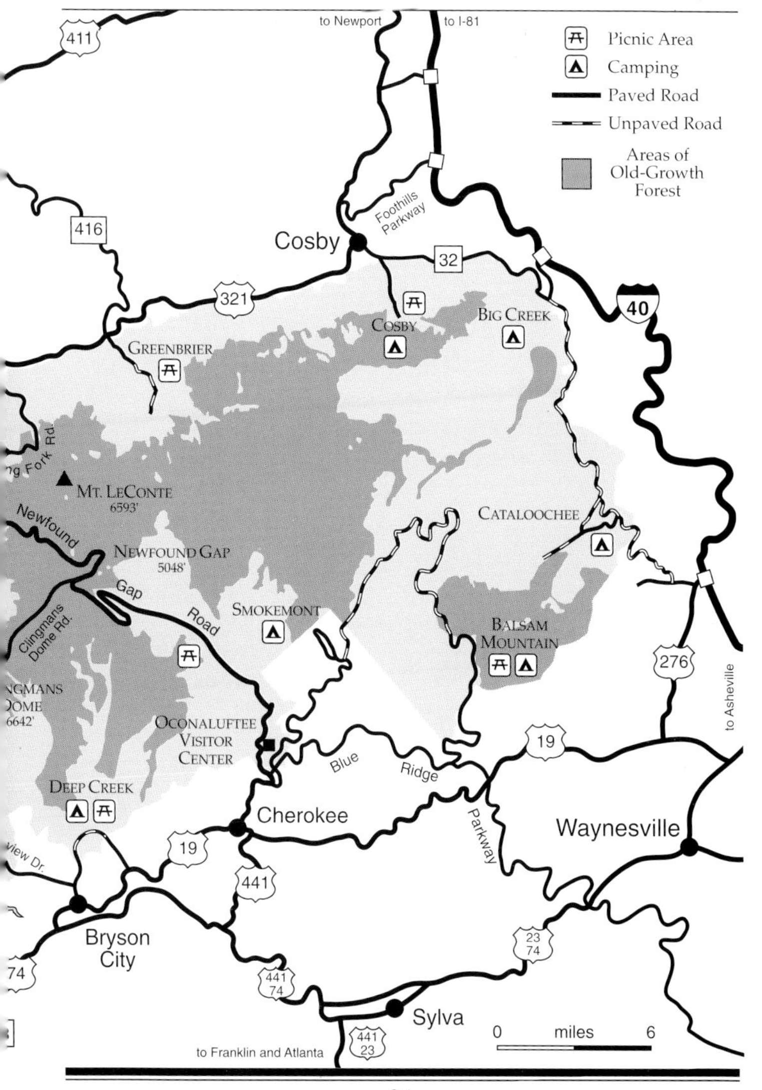

to Newport
to I-81
Picnic Area
Camping
Paved Road
Unpaved Road
Areas of Old-Growth Forest
411
416
Cosby
Foothills Parkway
32
321
40
Cosby
Big Creek
Greenbrier
Mt. LeConte 6593'
Newfound
Newfound Gap 5048'
Gap Road
Cataloochee
Clingmans Dome Rd.
Smokemont
Balsam Mountain
276
to Asheville
Oconaluftee Visitor Center
19
Blue Ridge Parkway
Deep Creek
Cherokee
Waynesville
19
441
Bryson City
23 74
74
441 74
Sylva
0 miles 6
441 23
to Franklin and Atlanta

A CHECKLIST FOR THE TREES OF GREAT SMOKY MOUNTAINS NATIONAL PARK

c=Common, f=Frequent
o=Occasional, i=Infrequent
s=Scarce, r=Rare, vr=Very Rare
lo=Low Elevations (850'-2,500')
mid=Middle Elevations (2,500'-4,500')
hi=High Elevations (4,500'-6,600')
wr=Wide Range of Elevations
hs=Homesites, *Non-native

TREES

- ☐ *Abies fraseri* Fraser fir c, hi
- ☐ *Acer leucoderme* chalk maple s, lo
- ☐ *Acer negundo* box-elder f, lo
- ☐ **Acer platanoides* Norway maple r, lo
- ☐ *Acer rubrum var. rubrum* red maple c, wr
- ☐ *Acer rubrum var. trilobum* trident maple i, lo
- ☐ *Acer saccharinum* silver maple s, hs
- ☐ *Acer saccharum* sugar maple c, wr
- ☐ *Aesculus flava* yellow buckeye c, wr
- ☐ **Ailanthus altissima* tree-of-heaven s, lo
- ☐ **Albizia julibrissin* mimosa f, lo
- ☐ *Betula alleghaniensis* yellow birch c, wr
- ☐ *Betula lenta* black or sweet birch f, lo-mid
- ☐ *Betula nigra* river birch o, lo-mid
- ☐ *Betula papyrifera var. cordifolia* heart-leaved paper birch or moùntain paper birch r, mid
- ☐ **Betula pendula* European weeping birch r, mid
- ☐ *Carpinus caroliniana* American hornbeam, iron wood or blue beech c, lo-mid
- ☐ *Carya alba* mockernut hickory c, lo-mid
- ☐ *Carya carolinae-septentrion alis* Carolina shagbark hickory s, lo
- ☐ *Carya cordiformis* bitternut hickory f, lo-mid
- ☐ *Carya glabra* pignut hickory c, lo-mid
- ☐ **Carya illinoinensis* pecan r, lo
- ☐ *Carya ovalis* sweet pignut hickory i, wr
- ☐ *Carya ovata* shagbark hickory s, lo-mid
- ☐ *Carya pallida* pale hickory s, lo
- ☐ *Castanea dentata* American chestnut f (root sprouts) wr

- ☐ **Castanea mollissima* Chinese chestnut r, lo-mid
- ☐ **Catalpa speciosa* Northern catalpa r, lo
- ☐ *Celtis laevigata* smooth hackberry r, lo
- ☐ *Celtis occidentalis* common hackberry r, lo
- ☐ *Cladrastis kentukea* yellow wood o, lo-mid
- ☐ *Diospyros virginiana* persimmon f, lo
- ☐ *Fagus grandifolia* American beech c, mid-hi
- ☐ *Fraxinus americana* white ash c, wr
- ☐ *Fraxinus pennsylvanica* green ash o, lo
- ☐ *Gleditsia triacanthos* honeylocust s, lo
- ☐ **Gymnocladus dioicus* Kentucky coffee-tree r, lo
- ☐ *Halesia carolina* silverbell c, lo-mid
- ☐ *Juglans cinerea* butternut i, lo-mid
- ☐ **Juglans mandshurica* Manchu walnut r, lo
- ☐ *Juglans nigra* black walnut f, lo-mid
- ☐ *Juniperus virginiana* red cedar o, lo
- ☐ *Liquidambar styraciflua* sweet gum c, lo
- ☐ *Liriodendron tulipifera* tulip-tree or yellow-poplar c, lo-mid
- ☐ *Magnolia acuminata* cucumber tree f, lo-mid
- ☐ *Magnolia fraseri* Fraser magnolia c, lo-mid
- ☐ **Magnolia grandiflora* Southern magnolia vr, lo
- ☐ *Magnolia macrophylla* big-leaved magnolia r, lo
- ☐ *Magnolia tripetala* umbrella magnolia c, lo-mid
- ☐ *Nyssa sylvatica* black gum c, lo-mid
- ☐ *Ostrya virginiana* hop-hornbeam o, lo-mid
- ☐ *Oxydendrum arboreum* sour wood c, lo-mid
- ☐ **Paulownia tomentosa* princess tree o, lo
- ☐ **Picea abies* Norway spruce s, wr
- ☐ *Picea rubens* red spruce c, hi
- ☐ *Pinus echinata* short-leaf pine o, lo-mid
- ☐ **Pinus palustris* long-leaf pine r, lo
- ☐ *Pinus pungens* Table Mountain pine c, mid
- ☐ *Pinus rigida* pitch pine c, lo-mid
- ☐ *Pinus strobus* white pine f, lo-mid
- ☐ *Pinus virginiana* Virginia or scrub pine c, lo-mid
- ☐ *Platanus occidentalis* sycamore c, lo-mid

- ☐ **Platycladus orientales* Oriental white cedar r, lo
- ☐ **Populus alba* silver poplar o, lo
- ☐ **Populus candicans* balm of Gilead r, lo
- ☐ **Populus canescens* gray poplar o, lo
- ☐ **Populus deltoides* Eastern cottonwood r, lo
- ☐ *Populus grandidentata* big-toothed aspen r, lo
- ☐ **Populus nigra* Lombardy poplar r, lo
- ☐ *Prunus pensylvanica* pin cherry c, mid-hi
- ☐ *Prunus serotina* black cherry c, wr
- ☐ *Quercus alba* white oak c, wr
- ☐ *Quercus coccinea* scarlet oak c, lo-mid
- ☐ *Quercus falcata* Southern red oak f, lo
- ☐ *Quercus imbricaria* shingle oak s, lo
- ☐ *Quercus marilandica* black jack oak i, lo
- ☐ *Quercus muhlenbergii* chinkapin oak s, lo-mid
- ☐ *Quercus muhlenbergii* f. alexanderi chinkapin oak r, lo
- ☐ **Quercus palustris* pin oak r, lo
- ☐ *Quercus prinus* chestnut oak c, lo-mid
- ☐ *Quercus rubra* Northern red oak c, wr
- ☐ *Quercus shumardii* shumard's oak r, lo
- ☐ *Quercus stellata* post oak i, lo
- ☐ *Quercus velutina* black oak c, lo-mid
- ☐ *Robinia pseudoacacia* black locust c, lo-mid
- ☐ **Salix alba* white willow r, lo
- ☐ **Salix babylonica* weeping willow r, lo
- ☐ **Salix caprea* goat willow r, lo
- ☐ *Salix caroliniana* Carolina willow r, lo
- ☐ *Salix nigra* black willow f, lo
- ☐ *Sassafras albidum* sassafras c, lo-mid
- ☐ **Thuja occidentalis* Northern white cedar r, lo
- ☐ *Tilia americana* American basswood r, mid
- ☐ *Tilia americana var. heterophylla* white basswood c, lo-mid
- ☐ *Tsuga canadensis* Eastern hemlock c, wr
- ☐ *Ulmus alata* winged elm c, lo
- ☐ *Ulmus americana* American elm f, lo
- ☐ *Ulmus rubra* slippery elm i, lo

SMALL TREES

- ☐ *Acer pensylvanicum* striped-maple c, wr
- ☐ *Acer spicatum* mountain

maple c, hi

☐ *Alnus serrulata* common alder f, lo-mid

☐ *Amelanchier arborea* hairy-leaved shadbush o, lo-mid

☐ *Amelanchier laevis* smooth shadbush c, lo-mid

☐ *Amelanchier sanguinea* round-leaved shadbush r, lo

☐ *Aralia spinosa* devil's walking stick f, lo-mid

☐ *Asimina triloba* paw-paw o, lo

☐ *Celtis tenuifolia* dwarf hackberry s, lo

☐ *Cercis canadensis* redbud o, lo

☐ *Cornus florida* flowering dogwood c, lo-mid

☐ *Crataegus calpodendron* limestone hawthorn s, lo

☐ *Crataegus crus-galli* cock-spur hawthorn i, lo-mid

☐ *Crataegus intricata* Biltmore's hawthorn i, lo

☐ *Crataegus macrosperma* scarlet hawthorn f, lo-mid

☐ *Crataegus pinetorum* hawthorn s, lo

☐ *Crataegus pruinosa* triangle-leaved hawthorn r, lo-mid

☐ *Crataegus punctata* round-leaved hawthorn r, lo

☐ *Hammamelis virginiana* witch-hazel c, lo-mid

☐ *Ilex opaca* American holly f, lo-mid

☐ **Maclura pomifera* osage-orange s, hs

☐ *Malus angustifolia* wild crabapple o, lo

☐ **Malus pumila* apple f, hs

☐ **Morus alba* white mulberry r, hs

☐ *Morus rubra* red mulberry f, lo

☐ *Prunus americana* wild plum o, lo

☐ *Prunus angustifolia* Chickasaw plum o, lo

☐ **Prunus avium* sweet cherry r, hs

☐ **Prunus cerasus* sour cherry r, hs

☐ *Prunus hortulana* hortulan plum o, lo

☐ **Prunus munsoniana* Munson plum o, hs

☐ **Prunus persica* peach s, hs

☐ **Prunus triloba* flowering almond r, hs

☐ *Ptelea trifoliata* Common hoptree r, lo

☐ **Pyrus communis* pear s, hs

☐ *Sorbus americana* American mountain ash c, hi

REFERENCES

Kartesz, J.T. A *Synonomized Checklist of the Vascular Flora of the United States, Canada, and Greenland*. Timber Press, Portland, OR. 1993.

FLOWERING DOGWOOD *Cornus florida*

Leaves:
3-5" long
(7.5-12.5 cm)
2-3" wide
(5-7.5 cm)

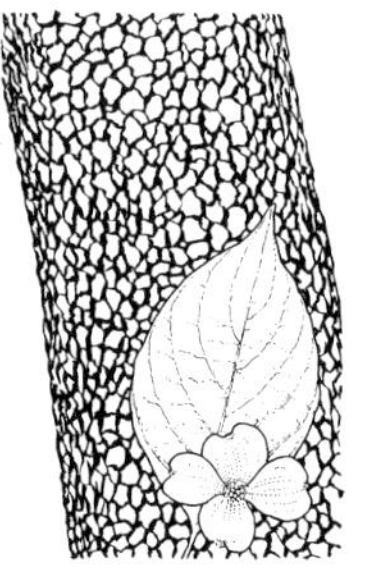

Flowering dogwood is easy to identify, even when not in flower. The leaves are opposite (growing directly across from each other on the twig). The unique bark is broken into tiny squares (1" or less across). The leaves have conspicuous veins which curve along a path mimicking the shape of the leaf. Bright red berries mature in September.

◆ **HABITAT**—Common below 3,000'.

◆ **SIGNIFICANCE**—*Horticulture* magazine dubbed this species "America's best-loved flowering tree." Large festivals are held each year in communities outside the park honoring the blooming, which in the Smokies, occurs from early April into May. Peak blooming is often around mid-April.

It's estimated that dogwoods produce an average of 20 pounds of berries per tree, which provide food for as many as 50 species of birds. Unfortunately, a non-native, fungus-caused disease called dogwood anthracnose is killing many park trees.

This tree's extremely hard wood was used by pioneers for horse collars, cogs for grist mills, and shuttles for weaving looms.

◆ **FALL COLOR**—deep red.

ALTERNATE-LEAVED DOGWOOD

Cornus alternifolia

Leaves:
3-5" long
(7.5-12.5 cm)
2-3" wide
(5-7.5 cm)

The leaves of this small tree resemble those of its more famous cousin, the flowering dogwood. But, as the name implies, the leaves of the alternate-leaved dogwood do not grow in pairs directly opposite from one another on the twig.

When young, the bark of the alternate-leaved dogwood is greenish with vertical white stripes. As the tree grows older, the bark often becomes brownish with horizontal cracks.

When this tree blooms in May and June, it lacks the big white flower petals (actually bracts) which are so notable on the flowering dogwood. Look for the alternate-leaved dogwood's green twigs and dark blue berries, the latter appearing in August and September.

◆ **HABITAT**—A frequent tree at all elevations, but may be more common at the mid- to high elevations.

◆ **SIGNIFICANCE**—In 1964, Park Naturalist Arthur Stupka reported an alternate-leaved dogwood 30' tall with a 12" circumference on the Gregory Ridge Trail.

◆ **FALL COLOR**—yellow or red.

Black Gum *Nyssa sylvatica*

Leaves:
2-5" long
5-12.5 cm
1-3" wide
2.5-7.5 cm

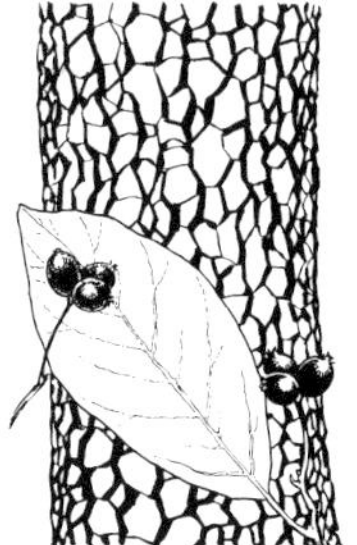

Black gum leaves have no teeth and look similar to persimmon leaves. Habitat and branches are the best identifying characteristics. Black gum branches are generally horizontal in relation to the trunk. Looking up at a black gum, it appears as if the leaves are arranged in a pinwheel form around the branches. Black gum leaves are also much glossier than persimmon leaves and they have a distinctly pointed tip. The bark is light gray and square-checked. Buds at the ends of the twigs are bullet-shaped.

◆ **HABITAT**— Black gum is most common in dry site oak and pine forests below 5,300'.

◆ **SIGNIFICANCE**—Bear, Ruffed Grouse, and Wild Turkey feast on the bluish-black fruits of this tree. Birds feeding on the fermented berries have been known to become disoriented and fly into buildings. Black gum wood resists splitting so well that some pioneers used it for ploughshares. Mountaineers made bee gums and food storage bins from hollow black gum logs.

◆ **FALL COLOR**—turns a noteworthy blood red in September, persisting into October.

Diospyros virginiana PERSIMMON

Leaves:
4-6" long
10-15 cm
2-3" wide
5-7.5 cm

The bark of this tree is one of the best identifying characteristics. It is dark and furrowed into distinctively thick, squarish or rectangular knobs. The leaves are completely toothless and have unusually broad, flat mid-ribs. The buds are extremely dark.

The famously sour fruit of this tree is round, 1-2" wide, and matures into a rich orange-red to purple color. Fruits appear in the fall, and only female trees bear them.

HABITAT—Frequent in well-drained, sandy soils below 2,500', especially around Cades Cove.

SIGNIFICANCE—The unripened fruit of this tree is so sour that the Cherokees called it *tsa-la-lu-i*, meaning "pucker mouth." Local connoisseurs say to wait until several hard frosts have passed before eating. Pioneers used the ripe fruits for salads, jellies, cakes, and custards. Bear, fox, raccoon, skunk, and opossum are also very fond of the fruit. The heartwood of this tree is extremely heavy (59 pounds per cubic foot) and has been used for golf club heads.

FALL COLOR—yellow, purple, orange, scarlet.

Paw-Paw

Asimina triloba

Leaves:
6-12" long
(15-30 cm)
2-4" wide
(5-10 cm)

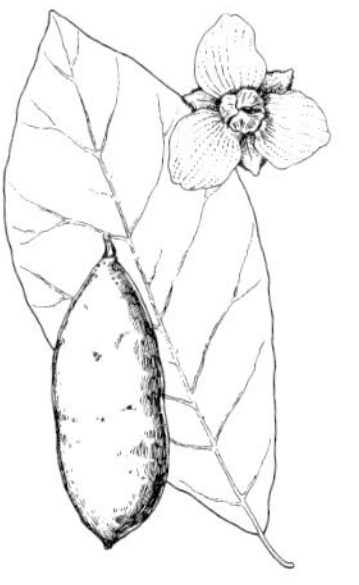

Everything about the paw-paw is unusual. Its large (6-12") leaves are thin and share a droopiness with several related tropical species. They are broadest above the middle. When crushed, the leaves sometimes exude an asphalt-like odor.

Paw-paw flowers are brown to maroon and have three outer petal-like structures called sepals and two whorls of three (six total) inner petals. The flowers appear before the leaves. The peculiar, banana-like fruits ripen in September. Many park trees, however, do not produce fruit. Paw-paws are often found in groups because they reproduce by root sprouts.

The bark of this species is thin and often marked with white blotches and numerous small bumps. The buds have brown hairs.

◆ **HABITAT**— A frequent species below 2,600', especially near streams.

◆ **SIGNIFICANCE**—Old-timers made bread and pudding from paw-paw fruits. The Cherokees used the bark to make string and rope. Opossum are also very fond of paw-paw fruits.

◆ **FALL COLOR**—yellow.

Magnolia acuminata

CUCUMBER TREE

Leaves:
6-10" long
(15-25 cm)
3-6" wide
(7.5-15 cm)

The leaves of this tree are smaller than the other magnolias in the park, but longer and broader than other trees with oval, untoothed leaves. There are usually fine hairs on the leaves' undersides and the bases of most leaves are U-shaped. The trunk of this tree is generally straight and has bark that sheds papery flakes when rubbed. Greenish-yellow, bell-shaped flowers bloom on cucumber trees in late April.

The common name for the cucumber tree comes from the fruits which appear in mid-summer. They are about 2" long, green and red, with a bumpy texture which makes them resemble cucumbers. When broken, the fruits produce a pleasant, pungent, spicy odor.

◆ **HABITAT**—A frequent species on rich soils below 5,000'.

◆ **SIGNIFICANCE**—The Cherokee name for this tree translates to "big leaves," which they used to treat toothaches. In the late 1950s, a tree with a circumference of 220" was recorded on the Kalanu Prong in the Greenbrier area. The national champion cucumber tree is 293" (24' 5") in circumference and grows in Waukon, Iowa.

Fraser Magnolia *Magnolia fraseri*

Leaves:
8-16" long
(20-40 cm)

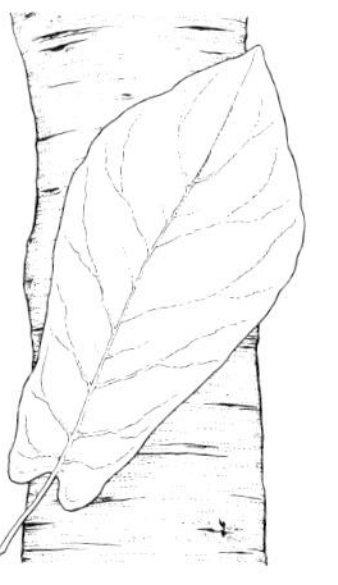

The size of the leaf (8-16") and the notch or "ears" at the base of the leaf may be all you need to identify this tree. The trunks of Fraser magnolias have smooth gray bark and often occur in clusters. Its twigs are very thick and have large, long-pointed buds. In late April and early May this tree displays big, creamy white flowers which appear at the same time as the leaves. The large fruits (3"-4" long) turn bright red in late July.

◆ **HABITAT**—Common in moist situations up to 5,000'.

◆ **SIGNIFICANCE**—This tree lives only in the southern Appalachians. Records show it was first identified by the famous botanist William Bartram in what is now north Georgia. Like many plants that live in the Smokies, however, it is named after the Scottish botanist John Fraser.

The Smokies are home to the national champion Fraser magnolia tree. It is over 120' tall and more than 9' in circumference. The champion is located near Albright Grove Loop Trail.

◆ **FALL COLOR**—gold to brown.

UMBRELLA MAGNOLIA

Magnolia tripetala

Leaves:
18-24" long
(45-60 cm)

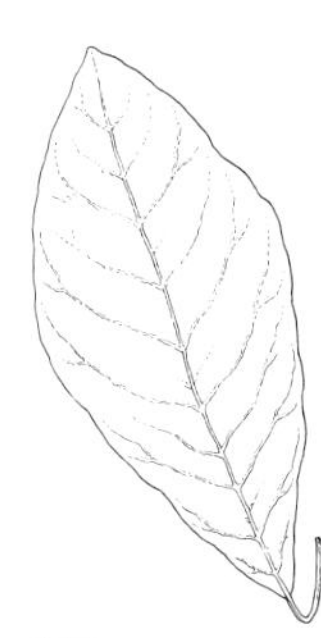

There is no missing the 18-24" long leaves of the umbrella magnolia. To discern it from a Fraser magnolia, just check the base of the leaf. The umbrella is pointed at both ends while the Fraser is distinctively notched at the stem. You might also note that the leaves on the umbrella magnolia all emerge from the branch at a different, spiralling angle, a bit like the spokes of an umbrella.

The bark is light gray and unusually smooth with many tiny bumps. This tree's big, creamy white flowers are conspicuous in May and you've probably noticed the big (3-4" long) bright red seed pods lying along the trail on your autumn rambles.

◆ **HABITAT**—Most common along streams below 2,500', especially along Little River and in Cades Cove.

◆ **SIGNIFICANCE**—The leaves of the umbrella magnolia are so large and heavy that they cause the tree's limbs to sag in summer.

The National Register of Big Trees lists the champ (which lives in Pennsylvania) as being 9' in circumference. However, the Smokies have the right habitat to be harboring an undiscovered champ.

ROSEBAY RHODODENDRON *Rhododendron maximum*

Leaves
4-10" long
(10-25 cm)
1½-3" wide
(4-7.5 cm)

Rosebay rhododendron leaves are generally narrower overall and more pointed at the ends than catawba rhododendron. Also, unlike the catawba, rosebay leaves are somewhat hairy underneath. Both shrubs have large, leathery, evergreen leaves that curl like cigars during periods of drought or cold. Rosebay leaves are generally 3-4 times longer than they are broad.

This large shrub or small tree flowers in June at the lower elevations and July at the mid-elevations. The flowers are usually white with greenish mottling, but are occasionally rose-pink.

◆ **HABITAT**—One of the park's most common shrubs from the lowest elevations to 5,000', especially in shaded ravines and near streams.

◆ **SIGNIFICANCE**—The Cherokees used this wood for carving pipes, spoons, and toys. They would also apply the leaves to their foreheads to treat headaches.

Rosebays with circumferences of 12-14" have been documented in the park. The world record specimen grows in Oconee County, South Carolina and has a circumference of 25".

CATAWBA RHODODENDRON

Rhododendron catawbiense

Leaves:
3-8" long
(7.5-20 cm)
1½-4" wide
(4-10 cm)

Both catawba and rosebay rhododendron have thick, leathery, long, evergreen leaves that are untoothed along the edges. However, the leaf of the catawba is often rounder at the base and tip and wider overall (about two times longer than wide). The undersides of catawba leaves are generally hairless.

Catawba flowers bloom in large clumps and are purple or pink.

◆ **HABITAT**—This is the rhododendron of the heath balds. It is most common above 3,500'.

◆ **SIGNIFICANCE**—One of the top 10 questions at park visitor centers (after where are the bathrooms? and where are the bears?) is "when do the rhododendrons bloom?" The catawba is usually at its peak along the Newfound Gap Road between June 5-15. Above 5,000', the peak is often between June 20-25. Good places to enjoy the show are Spence Field on the Appalachian Trail, the Alum Cave Bluff Trail, Andrews Bald, and the Inadu Knob area.

The abundance of rhododendron flowers varies markedly from year to year. For a time, botanists believed spectacular blooms occurred every 2-3 years, but now it appears to be entirely random.

MOUNTAIN LAUREL *Kalmia latifolia*

Leaves:
2-4" long
(5-10 cm)
¾-1¼" wide
(2-3 cm)

Along with the rhododendrons, mountain laurel is one of the park's grandest shrubs. It delights us by being both beautiful and abundant.

Mountain laurel's evergreen leaves are thick, leathery, untoothed, and pointed at both ends. They are green and shiny on top and olive-green on the undersides. Its pinkish, candy-striped flowers usually bloom from early May through June. Its fruits are round, dry capsules on a long stalk. Like some rhododendrons, the bountifulness of mountain laurel blooms seems to vary considerably from year to year.

◆ **HABITAT**—Common below 5,000', especially on dry, south-facing slopes, on heath balds, and in pine-oak forests.

◆ **SIGNIFICANCE**—The Cherokees nicknamed this species "spoonwood" because they carved spoons from it.

Many beekeepers believe honey made from mountain laurel flowers is poisonous. Livestock may also be affected by eating the leaves.

Park Naturalist Arthur Stupka documented a mountain laurel in the 1950s on Greenbrier Ridge with a circumference of 3' 6". Big tree hunter Will Blozan recorded a 25' tall specimen along Rabbit Creek.

Rhododendron calendulaceum

FLAME AZALEA

Leaves:
1-3" long
(2.5-7.5 cm)
½-1½" wide
(1-4 cm)

Flame azalea leaves are deciduous, pointed at both ends, and untoothed but hairy along the edges. The leaves and flowers are concentrated toward the ends of the branches. There should be some hairs on the twigs and on the undersides of the leaves. The flower and leaf buds are clustered at the tips of the branches.

Flame azalea's yellow to red flowers are considered by many to be the most beautiful of any wild plant. At the lower elevations, the first blossoms appear in late April. Flowers may linger into July on the balds at the higher elevations. As striking as they are visually, the flowers have no scent.

◆ **HABITAT**—Common from the lowest elevations up to 5,800', especially in pine-oak forests and on Andrews and Gregory balds.

◆ **SIGNIFICANCE**—In 1791, pioneer botanist William Bartram described this plant as "...certainly the most gay and brilliant flowering shrub yet known." Good places to enjoy it include Gregory Bald (late June to early July), Andrews Bald (early July), Thomas Divide Trail, Rich Mountain Trail, Schoolhouse Gap Trail, and the Chestnut Top Trail.

SWEETSHRUB *Calycanthus floridus*

Leaves:
3-6" long
(7.5-15 cm)
1-3" wide
(2.5-7.5 cm)

Sweetshrub leaves are thin, opposite (they grow in pairs directly opposite from each other on the twig) and rather spicy smelling when crushed. You should find soft hairs on the undersides of the leaves and on the twigs. When scratched, sweetshrub twigs are also spicy scented. This shrub rarely grows taller than 5'.

Attractive, fragrant, reddish-maroon flowers adorn sweetshrubs from mid-April into June. The fruits are conspicuous, 2-3" long, leathery brown pods containing many brown seeds.

◆ HABITAT—Common in moist areas below 3,500'.

◆ SIGNIFICANCE—According to local sources, the women of Cades Cove used to place the strongly aromatic flowers of this plant in their bosom as a perfume and deodorant. Such use gave rise to the nickname "bubby" (archaic form of boobie) bush. The scent of sweetshrub flowers is often likened to strawberries.

The Cherokees used sweetshrub seeds to poison wolves. The seeds are also said to be poisonous to livestock.

Lindera benzoin

SPICEBUSH

Leaves:
2-6" long
(5-15 cm)
1-3" wide
(2.5-7.5 cm)

Most people notice this shrub in the spring, when its small, bright yellow blossoms provide some of the year's first lively colors. Flowers appear as early as late February and may last through March.

Spicebush leaves are pointed at the base, have no teeth along the edges, are usually hairless, and appear well after the flowers. Unlike sweetshrub, they are alternate rather than opposite. Both leaves and twigs relinquish a strong, spicy, lemony scent when crushed or scratched. You can, in fact, identify this shrub just with your nose.

Bright red berries appear in autumn and change to black through the winter. They, too, have a spicy scent when crushed. Spicebush rarely grows taller than 15' in the park.

◆ **HABITAT**—One of the most common shrubs in the Smokies below 2,500'.

◆ **SIGNIFICANCE**—The Cherokees and white settlers made a light, lemony tea from the dried twigs of this shrub. Some people also used it for seasoning opossum and groundhog.

◆ **FALL COLOR**—gold or yellow.

REDBUD *Cercis canadensis*

Leaves:
3-5" long
& wide
(7.5-12.5 cm)

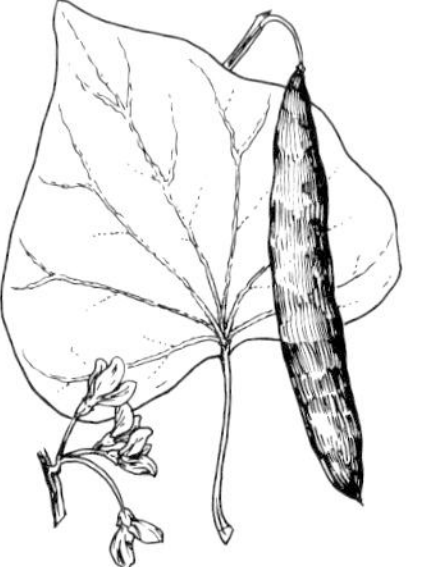

This small tree's beautifully heart-shaped leaves should be all you need to identify it. Basswood and some red mulberry leaves have a similar shape, but they are toothed along the edges. Also, redbud trees rarely grow taller than 30'.

The famous pink to magenta flowers bloom from mid-March to early April, before the tree's leaves appear. The fruits are about 3" long and look like rose-colored or brown string beans.

◆ **HABITAT**—An occasional tree on limestone-based soils below 2,000'. Such soils are found mostly on the west side of the park—especially along Rich Mountain Road, Cades Cove, the Laurel Creek Road, the Cosby area, and the Foothills Parkway between Townsend and Chilhowee Lake.

◆ **SIGNIFICANCE**—Cherokee children enjoyed eating redbud blossoms and adults made tea from the bark for treating whooping cough. In Mexico, fried redbud flowers are much revered.

◆ **FALL COLOR**—yellow.

Tilia americana var. heterophylla WHITE BASSWOOD

Leaves:
4-6" long
(10-15 cm)
2-3" wide
(5-7.5 cm)

White basswood's distinctively heart-shaped, asymmetrical leaves are finely toothed along the edges and whitish and hairy underneath. Numerous young shoots are commonly found growing from the bases of mature trees. The medium gray bark is thick and deeply furrowed, but has a smooth surface. Its unusual, winged fruit resembles a cluster of cherries attached by a long stem to a willow leaf.

◆ **HABITAT**—This species is common in the deep rich soils of the park's cove hardwood forests (3,000-5,000').

◆ **SIGNIFICANCE**—Bees swarm to the drooping yellow flowers of this tree when they bloom in early summer. Some people even say basswood honey is second only to sourwood for flavor. The Cherokees and others use basswood for carving and for making chair bottoms.

Pioneers hollowed out basswood logs and used them for vats and casks. Deer and grouse browse the tree's buds.

◆ **FALL COLOR**—light yellow.

AMERICAN CHESTNUT *Castanea dentata*

Leaves:
5-10" long
(12-25 cm)
2-3" wide
(4-7.5 cm)

The chestnut trees you see in the park today are root sprouts which persist from trees whose main trunk has died. These sprouts seldom grow larger than a few inches in diameter and 20-30' tall before they too, succumb to the non-native fungus which has killed an estimated 3.5 billion trees nationwide. The leaves of the chestnut are similar to beech leaves, but chestnut leaves are longer and have teeth that are larger and more sharply curved. The nuts of this tree are protected by very spiny husks.

◆ **HABITAT**—Once a dominant tree in cove hardwood and oak forests below 5,000'.

◆ **SIGNIFICANCE**—Because it resisted rot so well, chestnut was used by pioneers for fences, cabins, and outbuildings. Settlers in the Smokies gathered the nuts to sell. Moonshiners are said to have preferred chestnut wood for fuel because it produced little smoke.

Efforts have been underway for many years to breed a blight-resistant chestnut tree and restore it to the Appalachians. If you find any nut-bearing chestnut trees over 10" in diameter in the park, report their location to rangers at a visitor center.

Fagus grandifolia

AMERICAN BEECH

Leaves:
2-6" long
(5-15 cm)
2-3" wide
(5-7.5 cm)

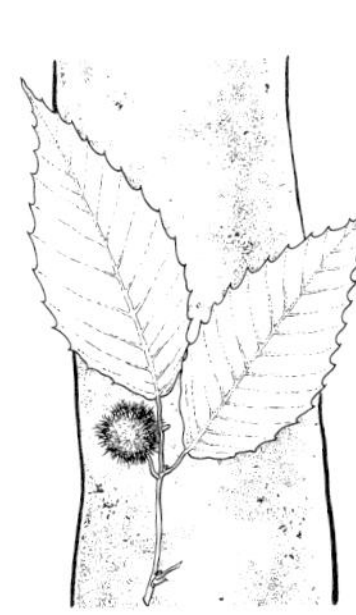

The best way to learn this tree is by the bark. It is smooth and steel-gray, though on some trees may be obscured by lichens, or, unfortunately, human carving. The leaves are thick, deeply furrowed at the veins and have teeth which are large, inward-curving, and prominent. Beech buds are extremely long and cigar-shaped, making them visible even at a distance. Many young beeches hold their dry, beige leaves throughout the winter.

◆ **HABITAT**—Common up to 5,800'. At the higher elevations it sometimes occurs in pure stands called "beech gaps." No one knows why these beech islands exist, but there is speculation that they produce chemicals which inhibit the growth of spruce and fir. In such gaps, beeches are often stunted.

◆ **SIGNIFICANCE**—Bear, deer, squirrels, turkey, and humans feast on beech nuts when they mature in August. Some native Americans believed beeches were never struck by lightning and so sought them out during storms. Even today, some people believe oils in the tree resist lightning strikes.

◆ **FALL COLOR**—yellow to orange-brown.

AMERICAN ELM *Ulmus americana*

Leaves:
3-5" long
(7.5-13 cm)
1-3" wide
(2.5-7.5 cm)

American elm leaves are distinctly lopsided at their bases and have doubly-toothed edges. They are 3-5" long (generally twice the size of winged elm leaves) and lack the ridged or "winged" twigs of the winged elm. The American elm's trunk is straight and unbranched (though sometimes split into two trunks at the base). Its bark becomes furrowed with age and may be broken into diamond-shaped ridges. The tree's twigs are generally hairless, unlike the slippery elm.

◆ **HABITAT**—A frequent tree below 2,200', mostly near streams and wet areas.

◆ **SIGNIFICANCE**—This tree is best known for the fungus which decimated it: the Dutch elm disease. The disease did not affect elms in the national park and other forested areas as much as trees in urban areas. Still, a few trees in the Smokies continue to succumb to the non-native fungus.

◆ **FALL COLOR**—pale yellow.

Ulmus alata

WINGED ELM

Leaves:
1½-2½" long
(4-6 cm)

The prominent ridges or "wings" on the fine twigs of this tree will help you identify it. Like the American elm, the winged elm's leaves are doubly-toothed and lopsided at the base. Winged elm leaves, however, are about half the length (2") of American elm. The bark of the winged elm has narrow, shallow fissures. Its fruit is winged and about the size of a dime.

◆ HABITAT—A common tree below 2,000 feet, either along streams or on drier slopes.

◆ SIGNIFICANCE—Winged elms are infrequently killed by the Dutch elm disease. Although it lacks substantial commercial value, its hard, heavy, close-grained wood is used for some hardwood lumber. At one time the fibrous inner bark was soaked and used for making rope.

◆ FALL COLOR—yellow.

YELLOW BIRCH *Betula alleghaniensis*

Leaves:
3-5" long
(7.5-13 cm)
1½-2½" wide
(4-6 cm)

With the exception of trees larger than 2' in circumference, the bark of this species is shiny, yellow or silvery in color, and peels off in shaggy, papery, horizontal curls. On the oldest trees, only the exposed roots and young branches may show this shiny, papery quality. Yellow birch leaves closely resemble those of the black birch and both species' foliage have a wintergreen odor when crushed. On yellow birch leaves, however, the side veins are often branched.

◆ **HABITAT**—One of the most common trees in the park from 3,500-5,000', but a few occur below 3,500'. A dominant tree in the upper elevation northern hardwood forests.

◆ **SIGNIFICANCE**—Mountain folk liked to use this wood for baking because it burns slow and gives off lots of heat. The curling peels of bark make good fire starters, even in wet weather.

For a few years the Smokies could claim the record yellow birch, a 14' 1" in circumference giant that grew on False Prong Gap in the Greenbrier area. The current world record tree grows on Deer Island, Maine and is a whopping 21' in circumference.

◆ **FALL COLOR**—yellow.

Betula lenta

BLACK OR SWEET BIRCH

Leaves:
2-5" long
(5-13 cm)
1½-3" wide
(4-7.5 cm)

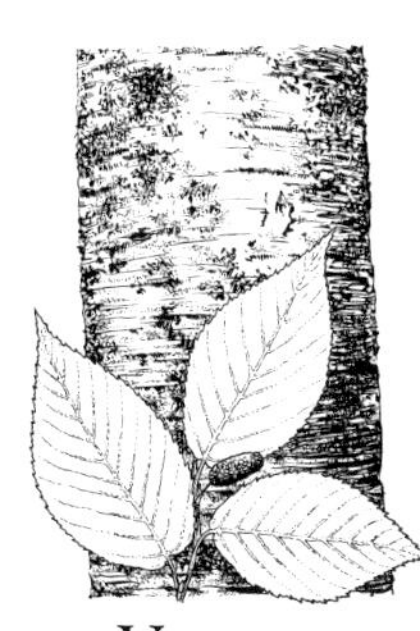

You can usually identify this tree by its tight, cherry-like bark and the very strong smell of its twigs when scratched. Although yellow birch may have a weak wintergreen scent, scratching a twig on a black birch releases an unmistakably bold wintergreen smell and taste.

Black birch bark rarely peels and is a shiny dark red color on young trees. There are horizontal streaks and scars on most young trunks and branches, while older trees develop heavy black bark. Black birch twigs are generally hairless, unlike most yellow birches.

◆ **HABITAT**—Frequent from 1,000-4,500'. Often associated with Eastern hemlock, sugar maple, American beech, and white oak.

◆ **SIGNIFICANCE**—Before artificial substitutes became available, black birch was the sole source of oil of wintergreen. Birch beer was made from mixing the sap with corn and other ingredients.

During the 1960s, a large tree with a circumference of 10' 10" was reported along Ramsay Prong on the trail to Ramsay Cascades. The champion of this species grows in New Boston, New Hampshire and has a circumference of 15'.

◆ **FALL COLOR**—bright yellow or gold.

RIVER BIRCH *Betula nigra*

1½-3" long
(4-7.5 cm)
1-2" wide
(2.5-5 cm)

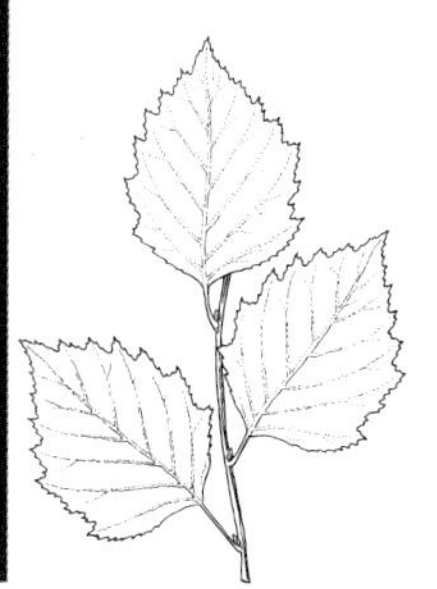

The bark of younger trees and branches peels off in shaggy, papery sheets which may be pinkish, buff, or reddish brown. Near the bases of older trees the bark is dark, rough, and deeply furrowed. River birch leaves have broader bases than other park birches and have sharply, doubly toothed edges and long, pointed tips. The buds, twigs, and leaf stems are hairy. Unlike yellow and black birches, there is no winter-green odor when you scratch the twigs.

◆ **HABITAT**—Found only at the very lowest elevations in the park, usually below 2,000'. Grows in wet areas, near the banks of larger streams and rivers. You can see it in Cades Cove, along lower Abrams Creek, and beside the lower Little River.

◆ **SIGNIFICANCE**—Because it often grows below the high water line of rivers and streams, this tree does an excellent job of stabilizing banks and reducing soil erosion. The wood of river birch has been used for dowels, toothpicks, and some furniture.

◆ **FALL COLOR**—pale yellow.

AMERICAN HORNBEAM *OR* IRONWOOD

Carpinus caroliniana
Leaves:
1-4" long
(2.5-10 cm)
1-2" wide
(2.5-5 cm)

The nickname "musclewood" aptly describes the distinctive form of this tree's trunk. If it has thin, smooth, grayish bark, and the twisted shape resembles a well-defined human arm or leg, there can be little doubt it's an American hornbeam.

The double-toothed leaves of this tree look much like yellow birch leaves, but are smaller (1-4"). Unlike the hop-hornbeam, the veins in the leaves of the American hornbeam do not fork. American hornbeam fruit will likely catch your eye in the fall. It grows in 2"-4" clusters which dangle from the branches like tiny Japanese lanterns.

◆ **HABITAT**—Common below 3,000', mostly beside streams and in ravines. A component of the cove hardwood forest.

◆ **SIGNIFICANCE**—American hornbeam or ironwood is legendary for its heaviness and toughness. Consequently, it was used for tool handles, levers, wedges, and the runners on pioneers' land sleds.

In the 1960s, a large American hornbeam (7' 7" in circumference) was reported in the Big Creek area. The record tree is 7' 11" in circumference and grows in Ulster County, New York.

◆ **FALL COLOR**—orange, red.

HOP-HORNBEAM *Ostrya virginiana*

Leaves:
3-5" long
(7.5-13 cm)
1-2" wide
(2.5-5 cm)

Chances are somewhat slim that you will see this small tree in the Smokies, especially outside the White Oak Sink or Cades Cove areas. If you do suspect you've found one, the bark and fruit are the most distinctive characteristics. The bark has a shredded look, being broken into narrow, vertical plates that are unattached at the bottom. The fruit is present from late summer through fall and resembles the hops from which beer is brewed (see illustration).

Hop-hornbeam leaves resemble American hornbeam and birch leaves. However, unlike the American hornbeam, some hop-hornbeam leaves have side veins which fork. (Bark will enable you to distinguish hop-hornbeam from the birches.) Hop-hornbeam rarely grows taller than 30'.

◆ **HABITAT**—Nowhere common, but most likely to be seen below 4,000' in limestone areas such as White Oak Sink and Cades Cove.

◆ **SIGNIFICANCE**—The Cherokees boiled the bark of this tree to treat tooth aches and sore muscles. Hop-hornbeam wood is heavy and strong and has been used for fence posts, levers, and cogs in machinery.

Smooth Shadbush or Serviceberry

Amelanchier laevis

Leaves:
3-5" long
(7.5-13 cm)
1-2½" wide
(2.5-6 cm)

Unlike the less common hairy-leaved shadbush (*Amelanchier arborea*), smooth shadbush has leaves that are hairless underneath. Both species have finely toothed leaves. Smooth shadbush often has smooth bark with dark, vertical streaks. Neither tree grows much taller than 30'.

The famous, star-like white flowers of smooth shadbush begin to bloom in late February or early March at the lower elevations. Grand displays of flowers have been noted on the "A.T." between Clingmans Dome and Silers Bald from May 10-15. When smooth shadbush blooms, the leaves are half unfurled and a reddish or bronze color. The tasty, purple fruits resemble tiny apples and are ripe by mid-June at the lower elevations, but not until August at the higher elevations.

◆ **HABITAT**—A common tree up to 6,000', especially in moist coves, near streams, and on grass balds.

◆ **SIGNIFICANCE**—Most old-timers agree that the common name "serviceberry" (sometimes called "sarvis") originated during the days of circuit riding preachers. The preachers would arrive in the spring, about the time this tree bloomed, and conduct the year's first service.

Sourwood *Oxydendrum arboreum*

Leaves:
3-6" long
(7.5-15 cm)
1-3" wide
(2.5-7.5 cm)

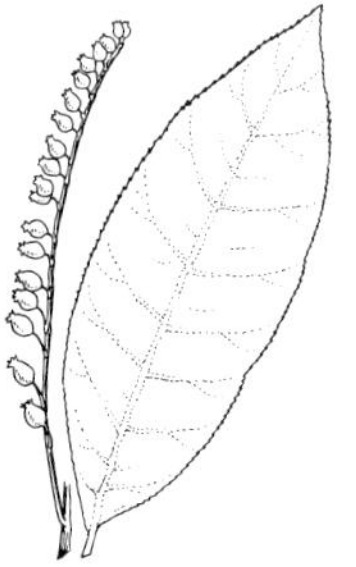

A good way to identify this tree is to taste a leaf. If it's very sour, as both the common and scientific names imply, it's a sourwood. The leaves are light green and have extremely fine teeth. They are similar to black cherry leaves, but the black cherry lacks the sour taste and has noticeably smoother bark. In July, the tiny, white, urn-shaped flowers of the sourwood are rather conspicuous. The cream-colored fruits grow in long, narrow clusters and remain on the tree throughout the winter. Its twigs are hairless.

◆ HABITAT—Common in dry oak and pine forests below 4,500'.

◆ SIGNIFICANCE—Mountain folks so valued the extraordinary honey that bees make from sourwood flowers that they avoided cutting the trees for fuel. Yet mountaineers did use the nicely curved wood for runners on their mule-drawn land sleds. You can see this arching, runner shape in many sourwood trunks.

The former national champion sourwood was discovered in the Smokies in 1994 by Will Blozan. It was 96' tall, 8' 8" in circumference, and lived near Snake Den Ridge Trail.

◆ FALL COLOR—a magnificent red which starts in late August.

Leaves:
3-7" long
(7.5-18 cm)
1½-3" wide
(4-7.5 cm)

More often than not it's the bark of this tree that reveals its identity. It tends to flake in rough, rectangular, purple or blue-black scales that bear a certain resemblance to a milk chocolate bar. Some naturalists, in fact, refer to this species as the "Hershey tree." When the tree is young, its bark is gray with light gray stripes.

Silverbell leaves are oval and fine-toothed, a characteristic shared with many other park trees. However, silverbell leaves are longer (3-7") than many other similarly shaped leaves, its teeth are extremely fine, and the tip of the leaf is sharply pointed.

The silverbell's lovely, name-sake flowers are conspicuous in April and May. The unusual, four-sided fruits appear in late summer and are seen on the ground throughout the winter.

◆ **HABITAT**—Common up to 5,000'.

◆ **SIGNIFICANCE**—The national champion silverbell tree lives in the park. It's 110' tall and 12' 7" in circumference.

◆ **FALL COLOR**—yellow.

Black Cherry *Prunus serotina*

At mid-elevations, the leaves of this tree can be confused with the leaves of the pin cherry or even sourwood. In general, however, pin cherry leaves are longer and narrower than black cherry and the teeth on black cherry leaves are larger and rounder. Black cherry leaves have hairs on their undersides along the mid-vein, while pin cherries are hairless. When young, both cherries have rather smooth reddish bark with conspicuous horizontal streaks. With age, their bark roughens. Mature black cherry bark resembles "burnt potato chips."

The black cherry grows considerably larger than the pin. Trunks of black cherries commonly reach 2-3' in diameter, while mature pin cherry trunks average about 1'. Black cherry fruit, which appears in September, is black; pin cherry fruits are red.

◆ **HABITAT**—Common below 5,000' in cove hardwood forests.

◆ **SIGNIFICANCE**—Black cherry may have been the most valuable tree to loggers during the pre-park lumber boom. Tent caterpillars prefer this tree for building their big webby tents and black bears often break off limbs to feed on the fruits.

◆ **FALL COLOR**—yellow to red.

Prunus pensylvanica

PIN CHERRY

Leaves:
3-5" long
(7.5-13 cm)
¾-1¼" wide
(2-3 cm)

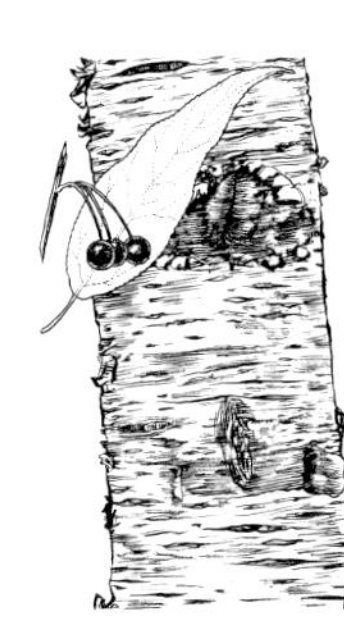

Pin cherry leaves are narrower and more sharply toothed than the black cherry. Pin cherry trees are also considerably smaller than black cherries. While black cherries may reach 50-60' tall, pin cherries seldom grow taller than 30' (see black cherry description). Pin cherry bark is smooth and reddish brown with horizontal streaks. The fruits are a brilliant, clear red. Both black and pin cherry leaves have two distinctive bumps (or "glands") near the base of their leaf stems.

This is a short-lived species and you may see as many fallen pin cherries in the park as live trees.

◆ **HABITAT**—Found mostly above 3,000'. Pin cherry is a pioneer tree which needs disturbance to become established. The presence of pin cherry trees (sometimes called fire cherry) is a sign that a forest fire, wind storm, logging, or other cataclysm has occurred at the site.

◆ **SIGNIFICANCE**—This is a northern species whose range extends down the peaks of the southern Appalachians from as far north as Hudson Bay. The small red fruits of this tree ripen in August and are eaten by bears and many species of birds.

◆ **FALL COLOR**—vivid pinkish-red.

MOUNTAIN HOLLY *Ilex montana*

Leaves:
3-6" long
(7.5-15 cm)
1-2" wide
(2.5-5 cm)

This large shrub or small tree may grow 15-25' tall. The leaves are sharply fine-toothed along the edges and long-pointed at the tip. They are thin and soft with conspicuous veins and midrib. Unlike the American holly, this species does lose its leaves in the fall.

Mountain holly's small (3/8" diameter), bright red berries appear on female trees in September. As the alternate name "winterberry" implies, they remain on the tree for several months. Mountain holly trees can be found across eastern America from Massachusetts to Louisiana.

◆ **HABITAT**—Most common above 4,000', although it does occur down to 2,000'. Often found on heath balds and other ridgetop sites.

◆ **SIGNIFICANCE**—In the 1960s, Park Naturalist Arthur Stupka documented a specimen 21" in circumference and 25' tall that grew near the Bote Mountain Trail.

Red squirrels are known to eat mountain holly berries.

◆ **FALL COLOR**—yellow.

Ilex opaca

AMERICAN HOLLY

Leaves:
2-4" long
(5-10 cm)

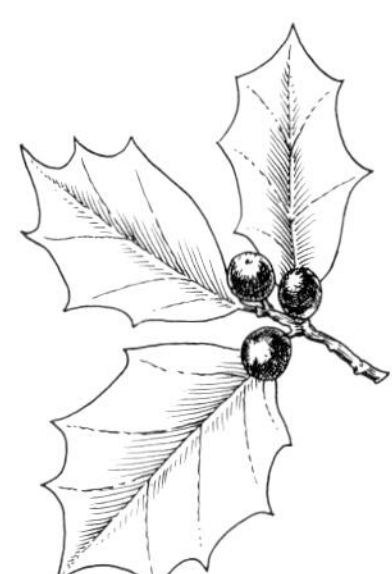

You can instantly identify this tree by its spiny, thick, glossy evergreen leaves which are well known from their role as Christmas decorations. No other tree or shrub in the Smokies has similar leaves.

American holly blooms from mid-May to early June. Its familiar red (green before ripening) berries can be found on female trees during much of the year. This tree's bark is smooth and gray.

◆ **HABITAT**—A frequent species in moist situations below 4,000'.

◆ **SIGNIFICANCE**—The Cherokees and other mountain folk carved stirring spoons from the wood of this tree. The ivory-white wood has also been used for piano and organ keys. In the early 1900s, many Christmas trees were American hollies.

Birds help propagate this tree by eating and dispersing its berries.

In 1934, an American holly with a 7' 4" circumference was reported on the Middle Prong of the Little River. Several very large trees also grow along the Russell Field Trail near Campsite 10. The world champion mountain holly lives in Chambers City, Alabama, and has a circumference of 9' 11". It's 74' tall.

COMMON ALDER *Alnus serrulata*

Leaves:
2-5" long
(5-13 cm)
1½-4" wide
(4-10 cm)

This is the only alder in the park. Its leaves have single or double rows of teeth and usually have hairy veins underneath. The bases of the leaves are more V-shaped than rounded. In the early spring, its dangling, finger-shaped, male flowers (called "catkins") can be quite conspicuous.

The common alder's fruits resemble tiny pine cones and are present most of the year. Like other alders, this species has a bushy shape with many trunks and stems. It rarely grows taller than 15'.

◆ **HABITAT**—A frequent species along streams, moist areas, and roads up to 3,000'.

◆ **SIGNIFICANCE**—This is one of the first woody plants to bloom in the spring, with some starting as early as mid-January.

Former Park Naturalist Arthur Stupka documented a common alder with a 22" circumference at the junction of Laurel Creek and the Bote Mountain Trail. All three national co-champion common alders can be found at the Riverside Business Park in Asheville, NC. The stoutest is 30" in circumference.

◆ **FALL COLOR**—reddish-brown.

Hamamelis virginiana

WITCH-HAZEL

Leaves:
3-6" long
(7.5-15 cm)
2-5" wide
(5-13 cm)

The waxy leaves of this small tree have wavy edges and characteristically uneven bases. Each leaf is nearly as broad as it is long. Witch-hazel's brown bark is often spotted.

This tree's unique, stringy yellow flowers appear from October through January, making it the first and last tree to bloom each calendar year. Its fruits are roundish, woody capsules which explode.

◆ **HABITAT**—Common in moist areas up to 4,500'.

◆ **SIGNIFICANCE**—From the days when the Cherokees were the only people in the Smokies, humans have rubbed bruises, scratches, burns, and sore muscles with an extract made from witch-hazel bark or leaves. Mountain folk of yesteryear and today have used divining rods cut from witch-hazel branches to locate water, gold, and graves.

Mischievous school children were known to bring witch-hazel seed pods into the classroom for the singular purpose of scaring their teacher and classmates when the unusual pods naturally exploded and flung their seeds 20 feet across the room.

◆ **FALL COLOR**—yellow.

Black Willow *Salix nigra*

Leaves:
3-6" long
(7.5-15 cm)
¼-¾" wide
(1-2 cm)

This is the only willow you are likely to see in the park and the only full-sized tree with extremely long, slender, non-compound (simple) leaves. The leaves have fine teeth along the edges and are green and hairless on both sides. Black willow flowers are about 2" long and droop like fuzzy yellow and green caterpillars. The bark is nearly black and on larger trees is thick and deeply furrowed.

A few non-native weeping willows grow in Cades Cove near homesites. Several willow shrubs occur throughout the park, including prairie, dwarf, and silky willow. The black willow is the only native willow over 30' tall you are likely to encounter here.

◆ **HABITAT**—A frequent streamside tree at the lower elevations. A few trees grow at the higher elevations.

◆ **SIGNIFICANCE**—White mountaineers and Cherokee Indians used the bark and twigs of this tree to make baskets. The Cherokees and other mountain folk drank tea made from black willow bark to treat headaches. Today, this bark is a source of salicylic acid which is used to make aspirin and other pain relievers. Black willow wood was once favored for the manufacture of artificial limbs.

Crataegus sp. HAWTHORN

Leaves:
1½-3" long
(4-7.5 cm)
1-2½" wide
(2.5-6 cm)

Most botanists agree that it is nearly impossible for anyone but a hawthorn specialist to reliably distinguish one species of hawthorn from another. Fortunately, the scarlet hawthorn (*Crataegus macrosperma)* is by far the most common hawthorn in the park, and consequently any hawthorn you see here is likely to be one.

As a group, hawthorns are fairly easy to identify. Their branches are close-packed and they have slender, very sharp thorns over 1" long. They are the only tree in the park with big thorns and simple (not compound) leaves. The thorns also lack buds and leaves.

The scarlet hawthorn produces ½" wide white flowers which bloom in early spring. Small, bright red, crabapple-like fruits appear in summer and may remain through the winter.

◆ **HABITAT**—Seems to be most common on the grassy balds, but is also found as low as 2,000' and in pine-oak forests.

◆ **SIGNIFICANCE**—Because of their thorns and dense structure, they have been grown to fence livestock. Shrikes (nicknamed butcher birds) impale their insect victims on this tree's thorns.

HOBBLEBUSH *OR* WITCH-HOBBLE *Viburnum lantanoides*

Leaves:
4-8" Long
& wide
(10-20 cm)

At the higher elevations, where this shrub thrives, there are not many similar plants to confuse it with. The big, roundish leaves have a distinctly rough texture, are finely toothed along the edges, and have prominent veins. The large clumps of white flowers that bloom in late April and May are both showy and attractive. The red, flat-topped fruit clusters last from late summer through fall. Hobblebush rarely grows taller than 8-10'.

◆ **HABITAT**—Occurs above 3,000'; becomes common above 4,500'.

◆ **SIGNIFICANCE**—Hobblebush often forms dense thickets which impede human travel. Some mountain folk would break off limbs of this shrub and hang them above their doors and chimneys to keep witches away. The idea behind this practice has been described as "anything that would hobble a human would hobble a witch."

◆ **FALL COLOR**—Perhaps the first shrub in the park to put on its autumn colors, sometimes as early as July. Peak of color is in September. Color ranges from yellow to red, and all shades may be seen on the same plant.

DOG-HOBBLE

Leaves:
3-6" long
(7.5-15 cm)
¾-2" wide
(2-5 cm)

This low, arching shrub has evergreen, leathery, rather shiny leaves that have small teeth along the edges and are pointed at the tips. From late summer through winter some leaves may turn to a maroon, bronze, or copper color. Its attractive, strongly-scented, bell-shaped white flowers bloom in clusters from late April to early June. The persistent fruits are dry, brown capsules. Dog-hobble rarely grows taller than waist-high.

◆ **HABITAT**—A frequent species at moist sites from 1,100-5,800'.

◆ **SIGNIFICANCE**—Dog-hobble lives only in the southern Appalachians. According to local lore, many bears have escaped pursuing hounds by dashing through dog-hobble thickets. Dogs apparently become hampered by the dense, low shrubs while bears are large and powerful enough to pass through them.

Mountain folk collected the colorful fall and winter leaves and used them for floral arrangements.

◆ **FALL COLOR**—bronze, maroon, copper.

Striped Maple *Acer pensylvanicum*

Leaves:
5-6" long
(13-15 cm)
4-5" wide
(10-13 cm)

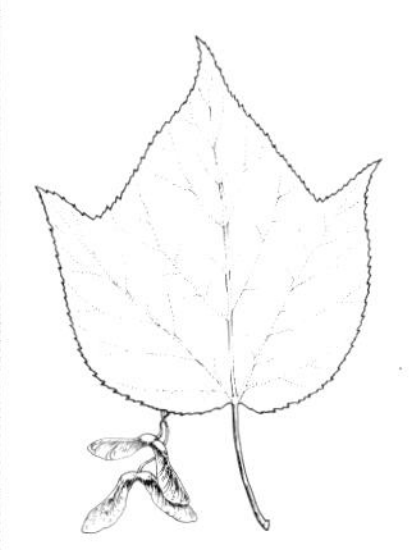

As the common name implies, this small tree has striped bark, especially when it's young. The stripes appear white against green. With age, the bark turns brown, but young twigs remain striped.

The nickname "goose foot maple" describes how the leaf resembles a goose's webbed foot. The three-lobed leaves have many very fine teeth, in contrast to the coarsely toothed leaves of the similar mountain maple. Also, the striped maple's twigs and buds are hairless while the mountain maple's are hairy. During April and May the drooping clusters of bright yellow striped maple flowers are very attractive.

◆ **HABITAT**—Common from the lowest elevations up to 5,000'. Usually an understory species.

◆ **SIGNIFICANCE**—Park Naturalist Arthur Stupka reported a 39" circumference tree off Pinnacle Lead. In 1997, big tree hunter Will Blozan discovered a national co-champion striped maple in the Smokies along Trillium Gap Trail. It's 77' tall; 44" in circumference.

Many botanists believe there are more large striped maples in the Smokies than anywhere else in its range.

◆ **FALL COLOR**—pale yellow.

Acer spicatum

MOUNTAIN MAPLE

Leaves:
4-5" long
& wide
(10-13 cm)

This alpine species closely resembles the striped maple, but lacks the vertically striped bark and has larger, rougher teeth along the edges of the leaves. Mountain maple leaves may have either three or five lobes, while the striped maple usually has just three. Also, mountain maple buds and twigs have velvety hairs, unlike the hairless striped maple. Its greenish-yellow flowers stand upright on their twigs like tiny candles when they bloom in June.

◆ **HABITAT**—Common from 3,000' to the highest elevations. Usually grows beneath larger trees.

◆ **SIGNIFICANCE**—During the early 1960s, a record mountain maple was recorded on the Trillium Gap Trail. It was 25' tall and had a circumference of 3'. The current champion tree grows in Houghton County, Michigan and is 2' 9" in circumference.

Mountain maple is a northern species which reaches the southern limit of its range in the Great Smokies and the mountains of north Georgia. North of the Smokies, the species does not usually grow large and is considered a shrub.

◆ **FALL COLOR**—orange to red.

RED MAPLE *Acer rubrum*

Leaves:
3-7" long
& wide
(7.5-18 cm)

Look for the V-shaped notch between the lobes of this tree's leaves to distinguish it from a sugar maple. Red maple leaves are also toothed along the edges, while sugar maples are smooth or only slightly toothed. The undersides of red maple leaves are more whitish than the undersides of mountain, striped, and most sugar maple leaves.

Younger trees have smooth gray bark with "moustache" shaped scars where limbs have broken off. Its bark becomes ridged on older trees. Red maples have red twigs, buds, flowers, and fruits.

◆ **HABITAT**—From lowest elevations to 6,000'. One of the most common trees in the Smokies.

◆ **SIGNIFICANCE**—The impressive flowers of this tree adorn the mountains in a wash of brilliant red from February through April. One Cherokee name for the tree means "blood-like."

White pioneers made black dye from the bark and made spinning wheels from the wood. In 1997, Will Blozan discovered the national champion red maple in the Smokies near the Maddron Bald Trail. It's a true giant—141' tall and 23' in circumference.

◆ **FALL COLOR**—Yellow to red.

Acer saccharum

SUGAR MAPLE

Leaves:
3-7" long
& wide
(7.5-18 cm)

Maples are some of the few trees in the park with opposite leaves (meaning leaves and twigs grow in pairs directly opposite from each other on the branch).

Sugar maple leaves generally have U-shaped notches between their 3-5 lobes. Many people use the "U" in the leaf and the "U" in the common name as a way of remembering this species. In contrast, red maples have V-shaped notches. Sugar maples have few if any coarse teeth along their edges, while red maples are usually double-toothed. Younger trees have rather smooth bark which becomes thick, furrowed, and shaggy on larger trees.

◆ **HABITAT**—Common below 5,000'.

◆ **SIGNIFICANCE**—It is believed that native Americans taught white settlers how to tap sugar maples for syrup. A good producing tree may yield 20 gallons of sap per year (½-¾ gallon of maple syrup). The park's Sugarlands Valley, between Sugarlands Visitor Center and Chimneys Picnic Area, was named for its many sugar maples.

◆ **FALL COLOR**—exuberant yellows and oranges.

MAPLE-LEAVED VIBURNUM

Viburnum acerifolium

Leaves: 3-5" long & wide (7.5-13 cm)

The leaves of this small shrub are opposite and similar to the striped and mountain maples' leaves. However, maple-leaved viburnum lacks the striped bark of the striped maple and grows at a lower elevation than the mountain maple. This shrub is also substantially shorter (rarely over 7' tall) than the other small trees. The undersides of maple-leaved viburnum leaves usually have velvety hairs and yellow or black dots. In May and early June you might notice this shrub's clusters of flat-topped, tiny white flowers which eventually mature into dark purple fruits. It has fine, black, hairy twigs with small buds.

◆ HABITAT—Common and widely distributed below 4,000'.

◆ SIGNIFICANCE—The Cherokees included parts of this shrub in a medicine used to treat smallpox.

◆ FALL COLOR—an unusual salmon to pink-magenta hue.

Leaves:
4-7" long
& wide
(10-18 cm)

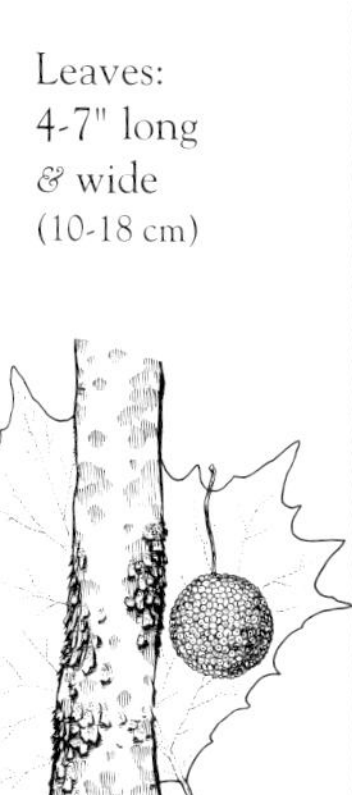

Chances are you can identify this large tree solely by its bark (or lack thereof). Unlike most trees, it sheds its bark as it grows. You may find big pieces of it on the ground and upon looking up notice the lime green or tan patches on the trunk where the bark has peeled off. "Sycamores look sick" (with their flaking patches of bark) is the way some people remember this tree. Its bare white trunk in winter has led it to be nicknamed the "ghost tree." The largest sycamore trunks, however, may be covered with brown bark, especially near the base.

Sycamore leaves are five-pointed and look a bit like some maple leaves, but they do not grow directly opposite from each other on the twig. Its unusual, long-stemmed fruits (often called "sycamore balls") may persist on the branches through much of the winter.

◆ **HABITAT**—Stream banks and moist areas below 3,000'.

◆ **SIGNIFICANCE**—In the right habitat this tree can grow to 150' tall and may live for over 500 years. Sycamores with circumferences of 17' 6" have been recorded in the park. Mountain folk made butcher's blocks from the wood and used hollow sections for grain bins.

TULIPTREE *OR* YELLOW-POPLAR *Liriodendron tulipifera*

Leaves: 4-6" long & wide (10-15 cm)

A good way to remember the name of this magnificent tree is by noting the resemblance of the middle section of its leaf to a tulip. Its common and scientific names, however, actually relate to its large (2" tall) green and orange flowers that drop to the forest floor in May. Its perfectly straight trunk and evenly-furrowed, light gray bark are usually sufficient in themselves for identification. Larger tuliptrees are often branchless for the first 30' or more.

◆ **HABITAT**— This tree is one of the most common in the park below 4,000.' It prefers rich, moist soils and often reclaims old fields.

◆ **SIGNIFICANCE**—These big, straight-growing trees were favored by mountain folk for building cabins, barns, and other structures. Little Greenbrier School, between Elkmont and Tremont, was built from 2' thick tuliptree timbers. The tree was also prized by loggers.

A truly mammoth specimen (over 25' in circumference) can be seen on the Albright Grove Loop Trail near Cosby, Tennessee. This is the largest tree in the park. The national champion tuliptree is 31' 2" in circumference and grows in Bedford, Virginia.

◆ **FALL COLOR**—yellow.

Liquidambar styraciflua

SWEETGUM

Leaves:
4-6" long
& wide
(10-15 cm)

The distinctively five-pointed, star-shaped leaves of this species allow you to identify the sweetgum at a glance. If you are still skeptical, crush a leaf between your fingers or scratch a twig for a pleasant, sweet, resinous odor. The bark of older trees is gray and deeply furrowed. Sweetgum twigs often have corky "wings" or ridges. The mature fruits are peculiar, 1" diameter, spiny balls referred to by some as "porcupine eggs."

◆ **HABITAT**—Common along streams and moist areas below 2,000'.

◆ **SIGNIFICANCE**—The Cherokees once harvested the sap of this tree and used it for chewing gum. During the 1930s, others sold the sap as "storax," a substance used in soaps, perfumes, and drugs. Sweetgum wood is very hard and heavy and is favored by cabinetmakers.

◆ **FALL COLOR**—extremely variable; from purple to yellow to red on the same tree.

SASSAFRAS *Sassafras albidum*

Leaves:
3-6" long
(7.5-15 cm)
2-4" wide
(5-10 cm)

Its amazing how much sassafras leaves vary in shape. They can be unlobed, mitten shaped, or have three lobes like a blunt-ended maple. Its spring flowers are yellow-green and the tree may sport attractive blue fruits in the fall. To confirm your identification, scratch and sniff a twig (which will be green). It should release a fruity or spicy smell. Crushed leaves are also fragrant.

◆ **HABITAT**—Common in old fields and other disturbed sites below 4,000'.

◆ **SIGNIFICANCE**—In the old days, root beer was flavored with the root bark of sassafras trees. Some optimists even believed sassafras to be a cure-all and it became one of Colonial America's first exports.

The Cherokee made tea from the roots to treat headaches and colds. Pioneers used the wood to make oxen yokes. Sassafras fruits, when they occur, are a favorite food for bear, deer, and many birds.

◆ **FALL COLOR**—yellow, crimson.

Morus rubra

RED MULBERRY

Leaves:
3-7" long
(7.5-18 cm)

Red mulberry leaves are always toothed and often lobed (the lobed leaves have a sassafras-like shape). Many, however, are symmetrically heart-shaped, rough textured, hairy underneath, and have distinctly pointed tips. The buds of this tree are green and the twigs are generally hairless. If you break the leaf stems, they should exude a milky sap.

Red mulberry's edible red and purple berries ripen in June.

◆ **HABITAT**—Found only at the lowest elevations (below 2,200'), especially around Cades Cove, Abrams Creek, Elkmont, and Greenbrier.

◆ **SIGNIFICANCE**—Though not the favorite berry of mountain folk, some did use the berries for jellies, pies, and wine. Even today, children in the know are big fans of mulberries.

Songbirds and many mammals gobble the berries and spread the seeds far and wide.

◆ **FALL COLOR**—yellow.

Northern Red Oak *Quercus rubra*

Leaves:
5-8" long
(13-20 cm)
3-5" wide
(7.5-13 cm)

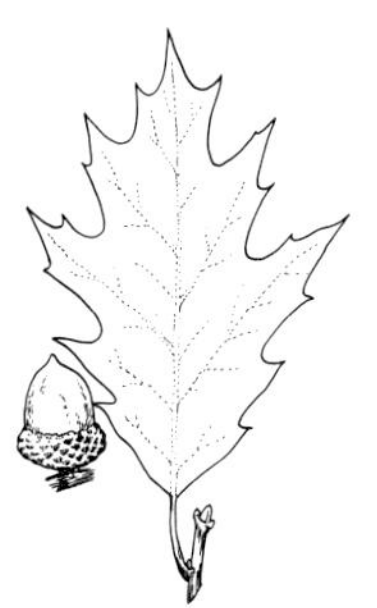

This is one of the largest oaks in the park, with some trees growing to over 100' high and 15' in circumference. Its leaves are less glossy on top than the similar black oak and are a yellow-green color. They are also thinner and less leathery than black oaks. The cap of the acorn is shallow, much shallower than the black oak. Its black bark may have shiny or silvery streaks in it. The end buds are hairless and angled.

◆ **HABITAT**—This is a very common oak, especially at mid-elevations on the North Carolina side of the park. It ranges from 1,500-6,000' and grows around the balds. Northern red oaks prefer moister sites than black, chestnut, and scarlet oaks. As the name suggests, this is a northern species common in Canada and the northern states.

◆ **SIGNIFICANCE**—This may be the most common oak in the park. Because it resists decay from sun and wind, pioneers used the wood for their split shingles. It's a fast-growing tree, up to a foot per year. There has been speculation that there are two distinct populations in the park—one at the high and one at the low elevations.

◆ **FALL COLOR**— dull red or orange.

Quercus velutina

BLACK OAK

Leaves:
5-9" long
(13-23 cm)
3-6" wide
(7.5-15 cm)

Because black oak leaves vary so much from tree to tree, and even from branch to branch, this can be a tough species to identify. Both the notches and the lobes of the leaves are variable.

Compared to the similar Northern red oak, the black oak's leaves are thicker, more leathery, and glossier on top. The buds on the ends of black oak twigs are hairy, unlike Northern red oak end buds.

Black oak is named for the distinctly black outer bark of mature trees. The inner bark, however, is yellow or orange. You can test this by scraping a twig with your thumbnail. The cap on its acorn covers about half the nut.

◆ **HABITAT**—This is one of the most common trees in the park on drier slopes at elevations below 4,500'. It grows alongside scarlet and chestnut oaks on south-facing slopes. Northern red oaks prefer slightly wetter situations.

◆ **SIGNIFICANCE**—The Cherokees made a tea from black oak bark for treating asthma. Black oak wood is some of the poorest of the oaks, but is used for some furniture and homebuilding.

◆ **FALL COLOR**—dull red or orange.

SCARLET OAK

Quercus coccinea

Leaves:
4-7" long
(10-18 cm)
3-5" wide
(7.5-13 cm)

The "C"-shaped notches in the leaves of this tree are deep, reaching nearly to the center vein. They also run approximately at right angles to this center axis. Each lobe has multiple, sharply-pointed bristle tips. Both tops and bottoms of the leaves are glossy and smooth (no hairs). The cap of the acorn covers about half the nut. The tip of the nut is often marked with circular lines. Scarlet oak twigs are hairless while the buds at the tips of the twigs are hairy.

◆ **HABITAT**—The scarlet oak is common on dry, piney slopes and ridges below 3,500'.

◆ **SIGNIFICANCE**—This tree is named for its brilliant fall color. For an oak, it grows remarkably fast. Blue jays and other birds are especially fond of its acorns.

◆ **FALL COLOR**—a brilliant scarlet. Its striking autumn appearance is often enhanced by the evergreen pines surrounding it.

Quercus falcata

SOUTHERN RED OAK

Leaves:
5-7" long
(13-18 cm)
3-5" wide
(7.5-13 cm)

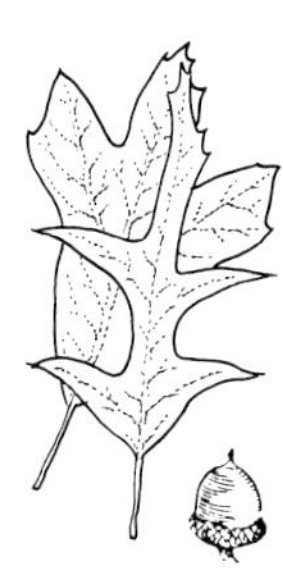

The leaves of this tree are highly variable and some may resemble the scarlet oak. Most Southern red oak leaves, however, have a long, narrow center lobe (sometimes called a "finger") which the scarlet oak lacks. Most Southern red oak leaves are divided into three major lobes. The upper sides of the leaves are glossy; the undersides are dull with felt-like hairs. Bases of Southern red oak leaves are usually strongly rounded. The twigs and buds are hairy. The acorn cups are very shallow, covering one-third or less of the nut.

◆ **HABITAT**—This species is not as common as the scarlet oak, being confined mostly to Cades Cove and other sites below 2,500'. It is usually found alongside other low elevation oaks and pines, especially scarlet oaks.

◆ **SIGNIFICANCE**—The wood of this tree is hard and heavy and is used for some general construction work.

◆ **FALL COLOR**— yellow-green to orange.

BLACKJACK OAK *Quercus marilandica*

Leaves:
3-5" long
(7.5-13 cm)
2-4" wide
(5-10 cm)

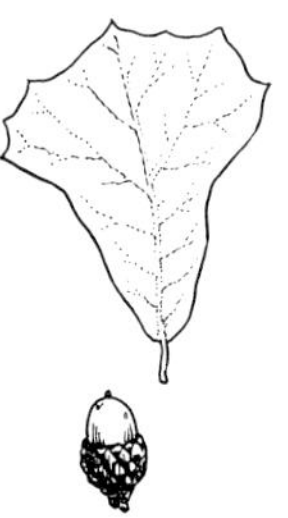

Blackjack oak leaves have narrow bases and very broad upper third sections. They are leathery in texture, glossy on top and have felty hairs underneath. Unlike the similar post oak, blackjack leaves have small spines at their tips. The acorns have bowl-shaped, very scaly caps that cover about half the nut. Blackjack oak bark is black with deep furrows and large plates.

◆ **HABITAT**—Prefers sunny, dry, rocky sites below 2,000'. Not common in the park except in the Cades Cove and Rich Mountain areas and around Fontana Lake. Often found growing with pines and post oak.

◆ **SIGNIFICANCE**—Blackjack oak is said to make wonderful firewood, but because of its small size, has little other commercial use. It is a pioneer species which often helps to stabilize and reclaim old fields and burned-over land.

◆ **FALL COLOR**— yellow to brown.

Quercus stellata

POST OAK

Leaves:
3-6" long
(7.5-15 cm)
2-4" wide
(5-10 cm)

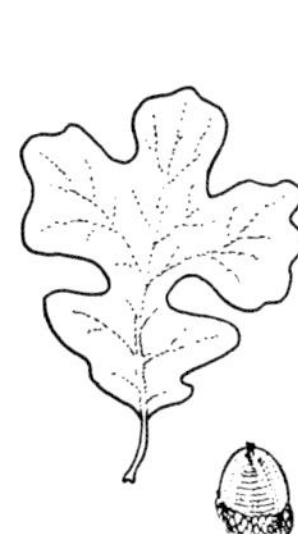

Post oaks have thick, leathery leaves with unusual, squarish lobes that often form a cross-like shape. The leaves' middle lobes are usually the largest. There are velvety hairs on the undersides of leaves and on twigs. The tops of the leaves are slick and glossy. The gaps between lobes are rounded. Post oak acorns are ½-1" long with a flat cup which covers about one-third of the nut.

◆ **HABITAT**—The only place you are very likely to see this tree is around Cades Cove, especially in the Cable Mill area and along the Rich Mountain Road. Post oaks prefer dry soils and exposed ridges below 3,000'.

◆ **SIGNIFICANCE**—Mountain folk liked to use this wood for wagon hubs, but its widest use was as fence posts (hence the common name). It is also said to make great firewood and to provide nutritious acorns for deer, turkey, raccoons, and squirrels.

WHITE OAK *Quercus alba*

Leaves:
5-9" long
(13-23 cm)
2-4" wide
(5-10 cm)

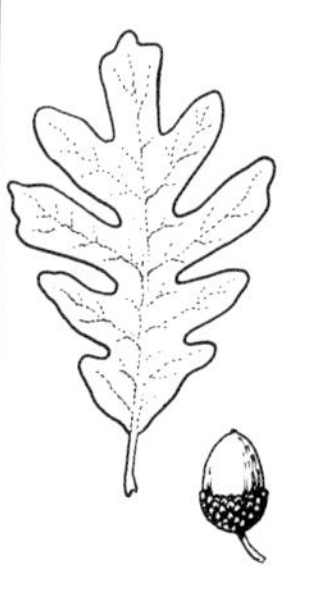

White oak leaves have smooth, rounded lobes which distinguish the tree from most other oaks. It could possibly be confused with the post oak (an infrequent tree in the park), but white oak leaves usually have 7-9 lobes, while post oaks typically have five. Also, white oak leaves are not thick and leathery like the leaves of a post oak.

White oak acorn cups cover one-third or less of the nut.

◆ **HABITAT**—White oaks prefer moister sites than most other oaks in the Smokies. They are most common at the lower elevations, but have been found up to 5,900'.

◆ **SIGNIFICANCE**—This tree is the oak of oaks: big, strong, and long-lived. White oaks over 300 years old grow in the park. Mountain folk used strips of white oak for baskets and chair bottoms. They also planted white oaks in their yards and many social gatherings were held in the shade of these splendid trees.

White oak has long been a preferred wood for furniture, cabinets, shingles, and lumber. Deer, bear, squirrels, and some birds are fond of its acorns.

◆ **FALL COLOR**— brown to yellow and red.

Quercus prinus

CHESTNUT OAK

Leaves:
5-8" long
(12-20 cm)
2-4" wide
(5-10 cm)

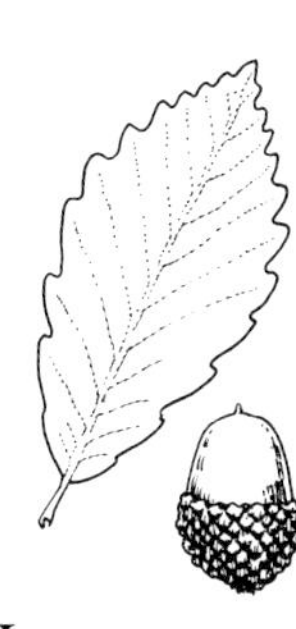

Like many trees that can tolerate dry, sunny sites, the leaves of the chestnut oak are fairly thick. They are glossy above and have wavy, rounded edges. The bark of mature trees is rough, dark, and deeply, asymmetrically furrowed with long, flat-topped ridges. Younger trees have a pinkish or salmon cast. Chestnut oak acorns are large with a warty cup that covers about half the nut.

◆ **HABITAT**— Pure stands of chestnut oak may be found on dry, rocky ridges below 4,000'. The tree also grows in sheltered forests, however, in competition with other hardwoods.

◆ **SIGNIFICANCE**—Chestnut oak is one of the major species which has replaced the American chestnut since the blight. The large acorn of the chestnut oak is eaten by deer, squirrel, and other wildlife.

The Cherokees used the tannin from the bark of this tree for tanning hides. Settlers and loggers later cut the tree on a fairly large scale for tannin. As white oak became scarce in the mountains, chestnut oak was used for railroad cross-ties and for furniture.

◆ **FALL COLOR**—yellow to bright crimson.

YELLOW BUCKEYE *Aesculus flava*

Leaflets:
4-7" long
(10-18 cm)
1-3" wide
(2.5-7.5 cm)

This is the only buckeye in the park and the only tree here with compound leaves consisting of five leaflets joined at the center. The toothed leaflets are connected like blades on a pinwheel. This is also one of the few trees in the park whose leaves (not leaflets) and twigs grow directly opposite from one another on the branch. Buckeye twigs are relatively thick and have large, bullet-shaped buds.

The bark is grayish brown and may become quite platy or shaggy on older trees. The familiar fruit is enclosed in a meaty husk. The nut is shiny, a rich brown color, and feels good in the palm of your hand.

◆ **HABITAT**—Prefers deep, rich soils from 1,000-6,300'.

◆ **SIGNIFICANCE**—The common name for this tree comes from settlers who likened the nut to the eye of a deer. Cherokee Indians carved ceremonial masks from the wood. This is one of the first trees to leaf out in the spring and to change colors in the fall. Big tree hunters Will Blozan and Michael Davie discovered the national champion yellow buckeye in the Smokies in 1995. It's 136' tall; 19' 1" in circumference and grows in the Cosby area.

◆ **FALL COLOR**—yellow to orange.

Acer negundo

BOX-ELDER

Leaflets:
2-4" long
(5-10 cm)
1-2" wide
(2.5-5 cm)

Box-elder is a member of the maple genus, but you'd never know it unless you saw the flowers or fruit. It has compound leaves with 3-5 leaflets per leaf. The leaflets often have very large, coarse teeth, especially the leaflet on the end of the leaf. Many leaves bear a startling resemblance to poison ivy, which is a woody vine. The twigs are distinctly green and hairless and grow in pairs directly opposite from one another on the branch. Younger trees and branches have smooth bark which becomes fissured and coarse with age.

◆ **HABITAT**—A frequent tree in the park, usually found below 2,000' near streams. Often associated with sycamores.

◆ **SIGNIFICANCE**—Evening grosbeaks and squirrels are fond of box-elder seeds. Pioneers made syrup from its sap and white sugar from the syrup. Because it often forks close to the ground, box-elder is usually passed over by timber cutters. The common name comes from the use of its soft, weak wood for making boxes. An alternative common name is the ashleaf maple.

◆ **FALL COLOR**—yellow or red.

BLACK LOCUST *Robinia pseudoacacia*

Leaflets:
1-2" long
(2.5-5 cm)
½-1" wide
(1-2.5 cm)

To identify this tree, look for the sizable (½" long) thorns which grow in pairs on the twigs. The thorns are not branched as they are on the similar, but much less-common, honey locust. The leaflets are rounder and their tips less pointed than on other trees with compound leaves in the park. The bark is rough textured and has extremely deep (1" or more) furrows. Whitish, fragrant, conspicuous flowers appear in April and May. During dry weather, you may have heard its 2-6" long, bean-like seed pods rattle in the wind.

◆ **HABITAT**—Common at low to middle elevations in disturbed areas and second growth forests.

◆ **SIGNIFICANCE**—Black locust wood is famous for its durability. The tree was so valuable to the Cherokees that they planted and cultivated it. They made blowgun darts, nails, and bows from the wood. Pioneers used locust for the base logs of their buildings and for fence posts because the wood resists rot.

Trees up to 13' in circumference have been recorded in the Smokies. The champion is 23' 4" and lives in New York.

◆ **FALL COLOR**— a pleasant, medium yellow.

Cladrastis kentukea

YELLOWWOOD

Leaflets:
2-4" long
(5-10 cm)
1-2" wide
(2.5-5 cm)

Yellowwood is one of the few trees in the park with compound leaves that have untoothed leaflets. The leaflets are also distinct for being arranged in an alternate, rather than opposite, pattern on the leaf. Each leaf has 5-11 leaflets. Yellowwood bark is very smooth, like a beech, but is usually darker or even black. Larger trees often have many root sprouts growing from their bases. Yellowwood limbs often branch from the main trunk with a U-shaped junction.

Tree lovers cherish the spectacularly heavy blooms of flowers which appear in May on these trees once every 3-5 years. The flowers are white, fragrant, and grow in heavy clusters somewhat like wisteria. Yellowwood fruits, which appear in autumn, resemble pea pods.

◆ **HABITAT**—Grows in rich, rocky coves from 1,750-3,500', but is nowhere very common. Several large yellowwoods grow in the Sugarlands Valley and along the Cove Hardwood Self-guiding Nature Trail, which starts at the Chimneys Picnic Area.

◆ **SIGNIFICANCE**—Pioneers boiled the roots of this tree to produce a yellow dye. This is the only tree of the genus *Cladrastis* native to America. All other relatives live in Asia.

WHITE ASH *Fraxinus americana*

Leaves:
3-5" long
(7.5-13 cm)
2-3½" wide
(5-9 cm)

This large tree has compound leaves with 5-9 (usually 7) leaflets. Each leaflet has extremely fine teeth, is 1.5 times as long as wide, and is green above and whitish underneath. Notice that the compound leaves grow directly opposite from one another on the twig. Its ashy-gray to brown bark is divided by furrows into a diamond-shaped or net-like pattern.

The very similar green ash is occasionally found at the lower elevations of the park, especially in wet areas. Green ash leaflets are often narrower (2 or 2.5 times as long as wide) than the white ash and are not as whitish underneath.

◆ **HABITAT**—Common in rich moist woodlands below 5,000'.

◆ **SIGNIFICANCE**—The Cherokees made a tonic from the inner bark of this tree to treat liver and stomach ailments. Pioneers occasionally used the tree for cabin building and made a yellow dye from the inner bark. Ash is often the wood of choice for tool handles, baseball bats, and oars because it is flexible. This is one of the few deciduous trees that the destructive, non-native gypsy moth does not eat.

◆ **FALL COLOR**—purple or yellow.

Juglans nigra

BLACK WALNUT

Leaflets:
2-4" long
(5-10 cm)
1-2" wide
(2.5-5 cm)

Like other trees with compound leaves, what looks like a leaf on this species is actually a leaflet. Consequently, the leaves of this tree are 1-2' long; the leaflets 2-4".

The single leaflet at the tip of black walnut leaves is often missing. When crushed, most leaflets produce a strong, spicy odor.

Black walnut bark is very dark and strongly ridged. The familiar nuts are about 2" round and covered with a meaty husk during summer and early fall. Black walnut twigs are quite stout.

Unlike the similar, but much less common butternut, the stems and twigs of the black walnut are not sticky. Also, butternut leaves usually have the end leaflets which black walnuts lack.

◆ **HABITAT**—Fairly common at old homesites below 3,500', but a few native, old-growth stands have been discovered in the park.

◆ **SIGNIFICANCE**—Mountaineers cherished black walnut wood for gunstocks, fence rails, barn beams, and waterwheels on mills. In pre-park days, it was common practice to plant black walnut trees around homes.

◆ **FALL COLOR**—light yellow to brown.

MOCKERNUT HICKORY *Carya alba*

Leaflets:
3-8" long
(7.5-20 cm)

Learning to tell one species of hickory from another can be challenging. The mockernut usually has seven leaflets on its compound leaf, but it can have nine, or, occasionally, five. If the leaflets are quite hairy underneath and have a strong aroma when crushed, chances are very good it's a mockernut. The stem which connects the leaflets should also be distinctly hairy and the twigs and buds are both stout. The bark is tight and furrowed. Mockernut nuts have thick shells and husks.

◆ **HABITAT**—A common tree in oak forests below 2,800', especially in Cades Cove and in the southwest corner of the park.

◆ **SIGNIFICANCE**—The Cherokee used hickory branches to make arrows and blowgun darts. Pioneers favored the wood for smoking pork and other meats in their smokehouses. The champion mockernut is a 11' 8" in circumference tree residing in Humphreys City, Mississippi.

◆ **FALL COLOR**—yellow.

Carya glabra

PIGNUT HICKORY

Leaflets:
3-6" long
(7.5-15 cm)
1-2½" wide
(2.5-7 cm)

The compound leaf of this species usually has five, but occasionally seven, leaflets. Unlike the mockernut hickory, the leaflets and stems are hairless. Pignut hickory bark is tight and dark with hard surfaces. Its twigs are slender and hairless. The pear-shaped nuts often stay closed, or they may open only part way.

◆ **HABITAT**—Common in dry oak forests up to 4,850'.

◆ **SIGNIFICANCE**—This tends to be the tallest hickory in the southern Appalachians. Trees 125' tall and 10' 10" in circumference have been documented in the park. The current national champion is 105' tall, 16' 8" in circumference, and lives on St. Simon Island, Ga.

Pioneers used hickory for making baskets, fences, wagon wheels, barrel hoops, and for those famous "hickory sticks" which maintained discipline in many classrooms.

◆ **FALL COLOR**—yellow.

Bitternut Hickory *Carya cordiformis*

Leaflets:
3-6" long
(7.5-15 cm)
¾"-1½" wide
(2-4 cm)

The compound leaf of this tree usually has seven or nine leaflets. The leaflets are narrower than on other hickories. You can identify this species by its conspicuous, sulfur-yellow buds which are present all year. The prominent bud at the end of each twig will be over ½" long. The shell of its bitter-tasting nut is quite thin and the nut itself is small. Bitternut hickory bark is relatively smooth compared to other hickories and is papery enough to flake if rubbed briskly.

◆ **HABITAT**—A frequent tree in well-drained soils below 3,000'.

◆ **SIGNIFICANCE**—Old-timers believed that if you cut hickory wood during January and February on the "old of the moon" that it stayed straight. The wood has long been favored for tool handles. Pioneers made yellow dye from the inner bark.

The former national champion was documented by Will Blozan and Bob Dellinger in the Smokies in 1997. It's 146' tall, 12' 9" in circumference, and is visible from the Porters Creek Trail. Bitternut is one of the fastest growing hickories.

◆ **FALL COLOR**—yellow.

Sorbus americana AMERICAN MOUNTAIN-ASH

Leaflets:
2-4" long
(5-10 cm)
½-1" wide
(1-2.5 cm)

The leaves of this small tree resemble a sumac. There are 11-17 narrow, pointy leaflets in each compound leaf. Each leaflet is 4-8 times longer than it is wide and has sharply toothed edges. Clumps of ½" wide, white flowers appear in mid-June, followed by striking, orange-red berries in September.

◆ **HABITAT**—Found only above 5,000' in the park. It's one of the dominant trees in the Clingmans Dome area. American mountain-ash grows in exposed and disturbed areas, often moving in where windstorms have downed other trees.

◆ **SIGNIFICANCE**—This is primarily a northern species which reaches the southern limit of its range in the Smokies. Bears are known to climb American mountain-ash trees to get to the berries. Songbirds are also fond of the attractive berries and reportedly become intoxicated from eating them. When the fruits appear in September, the fall colors at the high elevations will soon follow. A number of park trees are being defoliated by the non-native European mountain-ash sawfly.

◆ **FALL COLOR**—salmon-red or yellow.

Smooth Sumac

Rhus glabra

Leaflets:
2-5" long
(5-13 cm)
¾-2" wide
(2-5 cm)

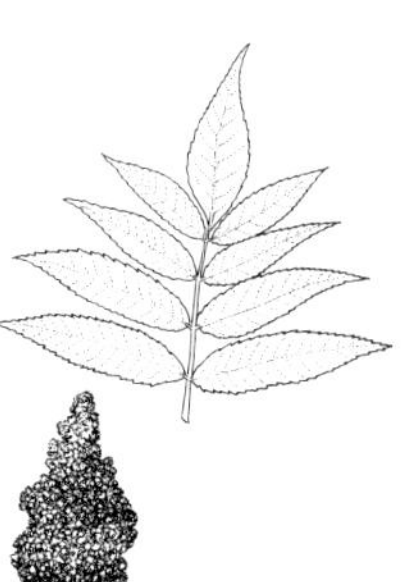

Smooth sumac is similar to staghorn sumac, except that smooth sumac has hairless or "smooth" twigs and leaf stems. Both of these sumacs have toothed leaflets on their compound leaves and lack the wings of shining sumac. The red, upright fruits of both are conspicuous in autumn. Smooth sumac occasionally reaches small tree stature in the southern Appalachians (15-20' tall).

◆ **HABITAT**—Common along forest edges, roadsides, and thickets below 4,000'.

◆ **SIGNIFICANCE**—The Cherokees gargled a tea made from the berries of this plant to treat tonsillitis. They also made a red dye from the berries.

Old-timers say that as children they made a lemon-aide type drink from the young berries. They also used sumac tubes for tapping maple trees for sugar.

When the light yellow flowers of this sumac appear in early summer, they attract swarms of nectar-loving bees.

◆ **FALL COLOR**—scarlet, yellow.

Rhus hirta

STAGHORN SUMAC

Leaflets:
2-5" long
(5-10 cm)
¾-2" wide
(2-5 cm)

Like the smooth sumac, staghorn sumac has toothed leaflets. However, staghorn sumac has noticeably hairy twigs and leaf stems which will help you differentiate it from smooth sumac. In addition, staghorn sumac lacks the ridges or "wings" along the leaf stems which the shining sumac sports.

The showy, bright red clumps of fruit (5-8" long) are conspicuous along roadsides in the late summer and early fall.

Of all the sumacs, this species is most likely to reach tree proportions, often growing to over 20' tall.

◆ **HABITAT**—Found along roads and in old fields up to 5,000'. It's slightly less common in the park than smooth sumac.

◆ **SIGNIFICANCE**—The common name "staghorn" describes how the hairy twigs resemble a deer's antlers in velvet.

In the early 1960s a staghorn sumac 25' tall and 35" in circumference was reported along the old Newfound Gap Road at an elevation of 3,600'.

◆ **FALL COLOR**—a showy red, purple, or orange.

SHINING OR WINGED SUMAC *Rhus copallinum*

You can identify this shrub by the odd-looking "wings" or ridges on the leaf stem between the slender leaflets. The twigs are about as thick as a pencil, velvety, and have many small, distinctive bumps. This is the only sumac commonly seen in the park with untoothed leaflets. In autumn, the red, hairy, drooping fruits are quite attractive. On some sites, this plant reaches tree-sized proportions (20' tall).

◆ **HABITAT**—Common along roadsides and other disturbed, sunny areas below 4,000'.

◆ **SIGNIFICANCE**—The Cherokees treated sunburn blisters by dousing them with a tea made from this plant. Robins, grosbeaks, bluebirds, and hermit thrushes are known to feed on winged sumac berries. In the early 1960s, an individual with a 13" circumference was reported along the Little River Road. The national champion of this species resides in Adams City, MS. It has a circumference of 40" and is 48' tall.

◆ **FALL COLOR**—bright red.

Aralia spinosa

DEVIL'S WALKING STICK

Leaflets:
2-3" long
(5-8 cm)
1½-2½" wide
(4-6 cm)

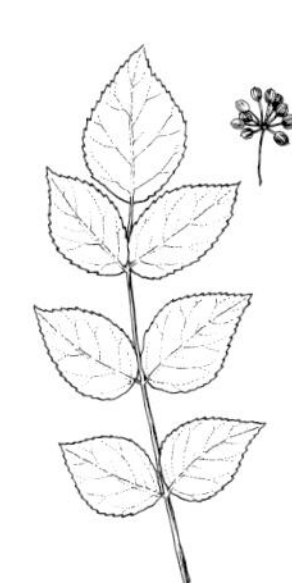

If, while hiking cross-country and climbing a steep slope, you mistakenly grasp the trunk of this small tree, you need no further assistance in identification. The short, sharp spines which cover the stems are both characteristic and truly memorable.

The small leaflets on the huge compound leaves are toothed, pointed at the tip, and dark green and smooth on top. The spines are present between leaflets and on the trunk and can be pushed off with your finger. Most leaves are crowded near the top of the tree.

During the latter part of July this small tree displays big, very conspicuous upright clusters of tiny white flowers which mature into blue or purple fruits by summer's end. Devil's walking stick often reproduces from root shoots and may multiply into dense clumps.

◆ **HABITAT**—A frequent species below 3,000', especially along roadsides and other areas which have been disturbed by fire, wind, or man. It does, however, grow in mature forests as well.

◆ **SIGNIFICANCE**—The Cherokees treated paralysis by bathing in the root ooze of this plant.

◆ **FALL COLOR**—light yellow.

FRASER FIR *Abies fraseri*

Needles:
$^3/_4$-$1^1/_2$" long
(2-4 cm)

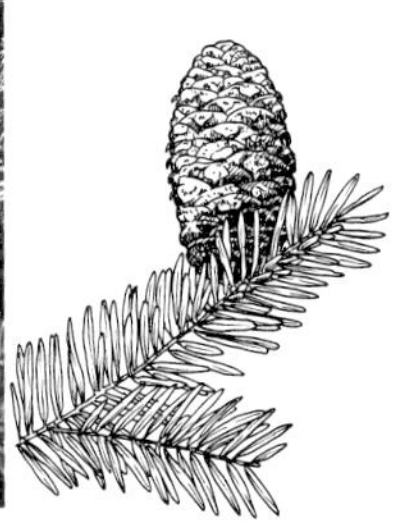

The needles of the Fraser fir are flat, fragrant, and friendly (they are blunt-tipped and won't prick you like red spruce or pine needles). At the mid-elevations, you could confuse this tree with a hemlock, but the latter has its needles arranged in a more open, irregular pattern on the branches. Also, hemlock needles are attached to their branches by tiny stems, while fir needles are stemless. Fraser fir cones stand upright on their branches (but cone crops occur only every 3-5 years). The bark is grayish brown and fairly smooth with many raised blisters.
◆ **HABITAT**—Found from 4,500-6,642'. Often associated with red spruce, but occurs in nearly pure stands at the highest elevations.
◆ **SIGNIFICANCE**—The Fraser fir has been decimated by a non-native insect called the balsam woolly adelgid. The tiny European insect, accidentally imported to the United States around 1908, has killed 95% of the mature trees in the park.

Fraser firs grow only in the southern Appalachians and 74% live in the park. Scientists are hoping that some Fraser firs will have a natural resistance to the adelgid and that they will pass on this resistance to offspring. Fraser firs are raised for Christmas trees outside the park.

Picea rubens

Red Spruce

Needles:
½" long
(1 cm)

You should have little trouble distinguishing this magnificent tree from other park conifers. The ½" long, square needles (one per bundle) lack the silvery undersides of Eastern hemlock and Fraser fir. The bark is flaky and the cones hang down from the branches. Tap the palm of your hand against the ends of the needles; if you feel the sting of their sharp tips, it's a red spruce.

◆ **HABITAT**—Grows down to 3,500', but is most common from 4,000-6,000'. Red spruce is not found west of Miry Ridge.

◆ **SIGNIFICANCE**—Both national co-champion red spruce trees reside in the park. The largest is 123' tall, 14' 1" in circumference, and grows in the vicinity of Breakneck Ridge.

Researchers in the Smokies are investigating widespread crown thinning and slowdown in growth of red spruce. Acid precipitation is the suspected culprit.

Red spruce is a preferred wood for Appalachian lap dulcimers. Millions of board feet were cut along the Smokies' ridgetops prior to park establishment. Spruce trees provide homes for the endangered Northern flying squirrel. Some park trees are over 300 years old.

RED CEDAR *Juniperus virginiana*

Leaves:
⅛-¼" long
(0.5 cm)

You should have little trouble identifying this evergreen tree by its small, scale-like leaves. The hard, green or blue, berry-like cones and the shredded outer bark are also characteristic. This is the only cedar or "juniper" in the park.

◆ **HABITAT**—Red cedars prefer limestone soils, which are rather scarce in the Smokies. Most of the limestone is concentrated at the west end of the park, especially in Cades Cove and Whiteoak Sink. The species is rather rare on the North Carolina side of the park. It's most common below 2,000'.

◆ **SIGNIFICANCE**—Cherokee Indians used red cedar for making furniture and moth-proofing their textiles. Cedar chests and blocks are still widely used for protecting clothing from moths.

Settlers in the Smokies liked to use cedar for building underground storage bins because it resists rot in contact with soil. They also used this fragrant species as Christmas trees.

Red cedar is the wood of choice for making pencils and the bark is famous as tinder for fire starting. Bobwhites, Mourning Doves, and many other birds eat the berries, especially in winter.

Tsuga canadensis

EASTERN HEMLOCK

Needles:
1/3-2/3" long
(1-2 cm)

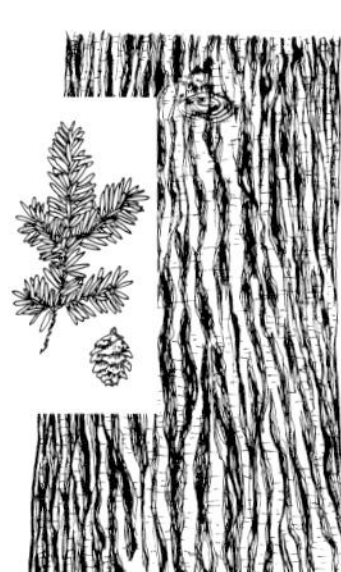

Park visitors often comment on the "lacy" appearance of these big evergreens. The needles are flat, soft, flexible, blunt-tipped, and have two pale lines on their undersides. They are much shorter (1/3-2/3" long) than the needles of any pine in the park and are not grouped in bundles. Hemlock may overlap with red spruce and Fraser fir above 3,500 or 4,000'. Look for the hemlock's persistent, tiny (1/2-3/4" long) cones and the thin stem at the base of each needle. Hemlock bark is characteristically thick and brown, becoming deeply furrowed.

◆ **HABITAT**—Common on north slopes and in ravines at the lower elevations and on ridges from 3,500-5,000'.

◆ **SIGNIFICANCE**—The national champion eastern hemlock resides in the park. It's a true giant—165' tall; 16' 8" in circumference. The tree was discovered by Will Blozan, John Boetsch, and Michael Davie in 1995.

Even during the turn-of-the-century logging boom, some hemlock groves were passed over entirely. An Asian insect, the hemlock woolly adelgid, is now killing many hemlocks in the park.

VIRGINIA PINE *Pinus virginiana*

Needles:
1½-3" long
(4-7.5 cm)

Of the five species of pine you are likely to see in the Smokies, three have needles that may occur in bundles of two (Virginia, Table Mountain, and short-leaf). The Virginia pine's needles are shorter (1½-3") and stiffer than the short-leaf pine's. The cones of the Virginia are smaller (1½-2½" tall) than the Table Mountain's and are not clustered in groups of three or more. Both Table Mountain and Virginia pine cones are, however, numerous and persistent. The bark of mature Virginia pines is broken into plates over four times as long as broad. In form, Virginia pines are often scraggly and shrub-like, hence the nickname "scrub pine."

◆ **HABITAT**—Common on poor soils and old fields below 3,000'.

◆ **SIGNIFICANCE**—The Cherokees made a tea from Virginia pine roots to treat sore throats. They use the needles for basket making and to scent soap. Though not a preferred wood, Virginia pine is used for pulp and fuel and is propagated to stabilize worn-out soils. Squirrels, turkey, and songbirds eat the seeds.

Pinus pungens

TABLE MOUNTAIN PINE

Needles:
1½-3" long
(4-7.5 cm)

Like the short-leaf and Virginia pine, the Table Mountain pine has two needles per bundle. The best way to distinguish the Table Mountain from the others is by its cones and habitat. The Table Mountain's cones grow in clusters of two or more and appear to be designed as deadly weapons. The closed cones are heavy, solid, and armed with stout, strongly curved, sharp spines which protect its seeds from wildlife. The cones are visible year-round, some staying on the tree for 20 years. The needles are straight, stiff, and sharp-pointed.

◆ **HABITAT**—Common between 3,000' and 4,500'. You are most likely to find it on dry, south-facing slopes and exposed, rocky ridges. At the higher elevations it is found in pure stands.

◆ **SIGNIFICANCE**—This picturesque tree grows only in the southern Appalachians. Although not especially large, it may live for 200 years. It is a symbol of long life and health to the Cherokees.

Experts suspect that this tree requires catastrophic fire for regeneration. Table Mountain pine cones explode during fires, scattering their seeds which survive best in mineral soils. Fire also destroys trees which compete with this pine.

SHORT-LEAF PINE *Pinus echinata*

Needles:
3-5" long
(7.5-13 cm)

This tall, straight pine may have either two or three needles per bundle. The needles are more flexible and a darker blue-green than the needles of the similar pitch pine (see pitch pine description). Short-leaf pine needles are also straighter than the twisted needles of the pitch pine. Even at a distance you can see its needles are much longer than Table Mountain or Virginia pine needles.

Short-leaf pines often lose their lower branches, even when young. Older trees may have very thick, reddish bark divided into rectangular plates by deep furrows and marked with tiny, crater-like pitch pockets. The narrow, egg-shaped cones which are usually present on the tree have short, thin prickles on their scales.

◆ **HABITAT**—An occasional tree on dry slopes and ridgetops up to 4,000'. May be more common at the west end of the park.

◆ **SIGNIFICANCE**—The straight trunk of this tree made it a favorite for building sailing ship masts in the days before steam power. Short-leaf pine is still widely used for lumber, pulp, and knotty pine trim. The Cherokees treated coughs with a tea made from its needles.

PITCH PINE

Needles:
3-6" long
(7.5-15 cm)

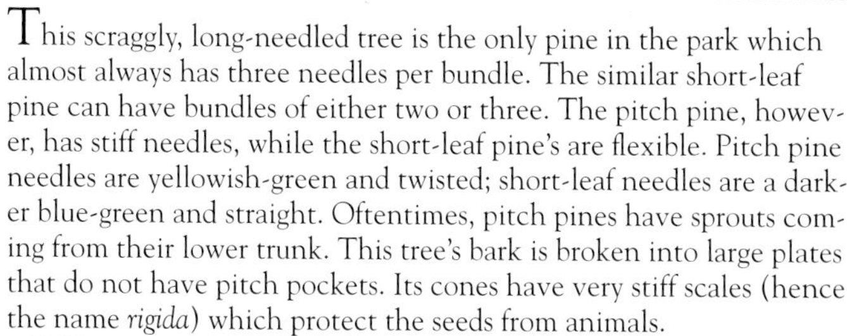

This scraggly, long-needled tree is the only pine in the park which almost always has three needles per bundle. The similar short-leaf pine can have bundles of either two or three. The pitch pine, however, has stiff needles, while the short-leaf pine's are flexible. Pitch pine needles are yellowish-green and twisted; short-leaf needles are a darker blue-green and straight. Oftentimes, pitch pines have sprouts coming from their lower trunk. This tree's bark is broken into large plates that do not have pitch pockets. Its cones have very stiff scales (hence the name *rigida*) which protect the seeds from animals.

◆ **HABITAT**—An occasional species below 4,000'. It is tenacious, growing in rocky, acid soils. Because it can not regenerate in shade, it is thought to be somewhat fire or disturbance dependent. Pitch pine often grows with Table Mountain pine.

◆ **SIGNIFICANCE**—Old-timers called this tree candlewood because the knots were burned as torches. A near record tree with a circumference of 9' 3" and a height of 82' used to grow in Elkmont Campground.

WHITE PINE *Pinus strobus*

Needles:
3-7" long
(7.5-18 cm)

This is the only pine in the Smokies with needles in groups of five (rarely four). The cones are open, loose, slender and very long (4-8"). This is also the largest pine in the park, with individuals reaching 100' tall and 10' in circumference. Branches grow out of the trunk at distinct "nodes" or growth joints.

◆ **HABITAT**—Grows on both north and south slopes, from the lowlands up to 5,000'. It is common in Cataloochee, where it was planted at the lower elevations by the Civilian Conservation Corps (CCC). Large white pines can be seen along the Cades Cove Self-guiding Nature Trail, just off the Cades Cove Loop Road.

◆ **SIGNIFICANCE**—White pine is a northern species which is more abundant in Maine and eastern Canada. It grows extremely fast and has been known to attain an age of 400 years or more. White pine lumber is so revered as a building material that very little virgin white pine forest remains today. In the past, when the tree was abundant, it was a preferred wood for building churches, homes, and mills. Red squirrels and Pine Siskins eat its seeds.

"The trees of America are the best God ever planted. Vast stretches of them have been cleared, but our forests still contain the largest, most varied, most fruitful, and most beautiful trees in the world."

—John Muir

KEYS

Keys to the trees and familiar shrubs of Great Smoky Mountains National Park

KEYS TO GENERA

When a genus is represented in the park by only one woody species, its full name is given in these keys to genera. If the genus has more than one species, only the generic name will be listed and the species will be found in the species keys that follow.

1. Evergreen trees or shrubs (leaves persisting into second year or longer; leaves broad, hard, leathery, or needle-like or scale-like)...2
1. Deciduous trees or shrubs (leaves of one year falling before the subsequent leaves expand)....3
   2. Trees with needle-like leaves or tiny scale-like leaves...Group A
   2. Trees with broad, hard, leathery leaves.....Group B
3. Thorn-bearing trees.....Group C
3. Trees or shrubs without thorns.....4
   4. Trees or shrubs with opposite leaves (two or more leaves at a node).....Group D
   4. Trees or shrubs with alternate leaves (leaves, leaf scars, lateral branches, and buds characteristically one at a node).....5
5. Leaves compound, (each leaf with distinct leaflets).....Group E
5. Leaves simple, sometimes deeply lobed, but never with distinct leaflets.....Group F

GROUP A

Key to the genera with needle- or scale-like leaves

1. Leaves needle-like, 2, 3, or 5 in a bundle with a sheath at the base, leaves 2" or more long ....*Pinus*
1. Leaves not in bundles, linear or scale-like, less than 2" long.....2

2. Leaves all small, scale-like, overlapping, the leafy twig more or less flattened.....3

2. Leaves not all small and scale-like, not on flattened twigs.....4

3. Branchlets vertically flattened; cone scales thick..............*Platycladus orientalis*

3. Branchlets horizontally flattened; cone scales not thick...........*Thuja occidentalis*

4. Leaves awl-shaped, tapering to a sharp point, or scale-like, tightly appressed to the stem....................................*Juniperus virginiana*

4. Leaves linear, spreading in one plane in all directions.....5

5. Leaves 4-angled, square in cross section, sharp-pointed; cones pendant..*Picea*

5. Leaves flattened, blunt, cones pendant or upright.....6

6. Leaves borne on stalks which persist on the twigs after the leaves have fallen; cones pendant........................*Tsuga canadensis*

6. Leaf stalks not persisting on twigs; cones erect...........*Abies fraseri*

GROUP B

Key to the genera of broad-leaf evergreens

1. Leaf-margins undulate, all with a few stout spinose teeth...*Ilex opaca*

1. Leaf-margins entire or with small teeth.....2

2. Twigs encircled by a stipule scar at each node; fruit a cone ....*Magnolia grandiflora*

2. Twigs not encircled by stipule scars.....3

3. Leaf-blades averaging more than 4" long......................*Rhododendron*

3. Leaf-blades averaging less than 4" long.......................*Kalmia latifolia*

GROUP C

Key to the genera of trees with thorns on the stem

1. Leaves compound.....2

1. Leaves simple.....4

2. Leaves all pinnately compound (once pinnate)................*Robinia pseudoacacia*

2. Leaves at least in part decompound (more than once pinnate) 3

3. Leaves very large (1½-4' long) bipinnate to tripinnate, borne in a cluster at the top of very stout stem; thorns weak, simple .....*Aralia spinosa*

3. Leaves smaller (less than 1' long), pinnate to bipinnate, scattered on the twigs; thorns stout, frequently branched ...*Gleditsia triacanthos*

4. Leaves untoothed (entire) ....*Maclura pomifera*

4. Leaves variously toothed, sometimes lobed.....5

5. Twigs typically stout, over ⅛" in diameter; the spur branches which are prolonged into thorns but little differentiated and often bearing leaves; leaves not deeply lobed..................................*Pyrus communis*

5. Twigs typically slender, less than ⅛" in diameter; thorns differentiated, stiff and sharp; leaves often deeply lobed...............*Crataegus*

GROUP D

Key to the genera with two or more leaves at a node

1. Leaves compound.....2

1. Leaves simple.....4

2. Leaves palmately compound (leaflets clustered at the apex of the petiole)..*Aesculus flava*

2. Leaves pinnately compound or trifoliate.....3

3. Leaflets 3-5, coarsely toothed toward the apex; fruit double-winged...*Acer negundo*

3. Leaflets commonly 7-11, entire or finely toothed; fruit single-winged...*Fraxinus*

4. Leaves characteristically whorled (3 at a node)....*Catalpa speciosa*

4. Leaves characteristically opposite, seldom whorled.....5

5. Leaves heart-shaped, large (6-12" long); exotic tree of city plantings, frequently escaped.............................*Paulownia tomentosa*

5. Leaves not heart-shaped, smaller.....6

6. Leaves entire or obscurely serrate or crenulate near the apex.....7
6. Leaves toothed or toothed and lobed.....8
7. Leaves with upper two veins strongly incurving; flowers surrounded by four large, white bracts; fruits are clustered drupes....*Cornus florida*
7. Leaves with two upper veins ending in leaf margin; leaves aromatic when crushed; flowers purple-brown, with associated bracts; fruit an aggregate of achenes..........................*Calycanthus floridus var. glaucus*
8. Flower clusters terminal compound cymes; fruits drupes; young petioles scurfy...*Viburnum*
8. Flower clusters axillary racemes, panicles or umbellate fascicles; fruits double samaras; young petioles smooth or hairy.............*Acer*

GROUP E

Key to the genera with alternate compound leaves

1. Leaves pinnately compound (once-pinnate).....3
1. Leaves decompound (more than once-pinnate).....2
2. Leaflets oval, about 5 pairs to each pinna; pod large, heavy (4-10" long); pith orange or salmon-colored.......*Gymnocladus dioicus*
2. Leaflets one-sided, about 20-25 pairs to each pinna; pod flat, thin (2-4" long); pith white..*Albizia julibrissin*
3. Leaves with glands on lower teeth, often with offensive odor when crushed..*Ailanthus altissima*
3. Leaves without such glands.....4
4. Leaves with odor of green walnuts when crushed; pith chambered..*Juglans*
4. Leaves without walnut odor; pith not chambered.....5
5. Leaves with pulvini; fruit a legume.....6
5. Leaves without pulvini; fruit not a legume.....7
6. Leaflets all opposite ....*Robinia pseudoacacia*
6. Leaflets mostly alternate ....*Cladrastis kentuckea*
7. Stipules or stipule scars present; buds red; vein-scars 3 or 5
....*Sorbus americana*

7. Stipules absent; buds not red; vein scars more numerous.....8
   8. Lateral buds partially or wholly concealed by petioles; fruit a small dry drupe; pith large..*Rhus*
   8. Lateral buds not concealed by petioles; fruit a nut, husk splitting along 4 lines; pith small, angled...*Carya*

GROUP F

Key to the genera with alternate simple leaves

1. Leaves strictly entire (never more than gently undulate).....2
1. Leaves variously toothed or lobed or both.....10
   2. Leaves heart-shaped ....*Cercis canadensis*
   2. Leaves not heart-shaped 3
3. Leaves mostly more than 8" long.....4
3. Leaves mostly less than 6" long.....5
   4. Twigs encircled by a stipular scar at each node ....*Magnolia*
   4. Twigs without stipule scars....................................*Asimina triloba*
5. Leaves characteristically clustered at tips of twigs with very short internodes; fruit a capsule.......6
5. Internodes not markedly shortened at branch tips; only one leaf at tip of each elongate vegetative branch; fruit a drupe or berry.....7
   6. Shrubs; fruit a capsule...*Rhododendron*
   6. Trees; fruit an acorn...*Quercus imbricaria*
7. Leaves with the upper 2 lateral veins strongly incurving ....*Cornus alternifolia*
7. Leaves strictly pinnately-veined to the tip 8
   8. Twigs and leaves spicy-aromatic ....*Lindera benzoin*
   8. Twigs and leaves not spicy-aromatic......9
9. Pith diaphragmed, but solid; vein scars 3..................*Nyssa sylvatica*
9. Pith sometimes with cavities, but not diaphragmed; vein scar one ....*Diospyros virginiana*
   10. Leaf-blade usually averaging at least 1.5 times as long as broad....19
   10. Leaf-blade usually about as broad as long.....11
11. Leaves more or less regularly toothed, but not lobed.....16
11. Leaves usually with a few conspicuous lobes, toothed or entire...12

12. Leaves bilaterally and symmetrically lobed.....14
12. Some leaves unlobed, others asymmetrically lobed.....13
13. Leaves coarsely serrate; fruit a multiple "berry"......................*Morus*
13. Leaves not serrate; fruit a drupe.............................*Sassafras albidum*
14. Leaf-tip truncate or broadly notched; leaves with one pair of broad, acute, lateral lobes..................................*Liriodendron tulipifera*
14. Leaf-tip acuminate; leaves with main veins and lobes essentially palmate......15
15. Leaves star-shaped with deep notches between lobes, margin with fine, regular serrations..........................*Liquidambar styraciflua*
15. Leaves not star-shaped, with shallow sinuses; margins entire except for a few sinuate teeth...........................*Platanus occidentalis*
16. Leaf-margins merely undulate or crenate; axillary buds stalked ....*Hamamelis virginiana*
16. Leaf-margins distinctly toothed; buds not stalked......17
17. Leaves all unlobed in Smokies' species, smooth above; sap not milky.....18
17. Trees usually with some irregularly lobed leaves but occasionally all unlobed; leaves usually somewhat rough above; sap milky; fruit multiple...*Morus*
18. Leaves in 2 rows; pith cylindrical......*Tilia americana var. heterophylla*
18. Leaves in more than 2 rows; pith 5-angled.......................*Populus*
19. Leaves characteristically clustered at tips of twigs, with very short internodes, prominently lobed or coarsely and regularly toothed; pith 5-angled; fruit an acorn................................*Quercus*
19. Leaves not characteristically clustered at tips except on spur branches; if somewhat clustered, with glandular petioles; if somewhat lobed, less than 3" long; pith cylindrical; fruit not an acorn.....20
20. Sap milky; fruit multiple and fleshy; leaves ovate to cordate ....occasional forms of *Morus*
20. Sap not milky; fruit not multiple and fleshy; leaves ovate to lanceolate.....21
21. Teeth of leaf-margins bristle-tipped.......................*Castanea dentata*
21. Teeth of leaf-margins not bristle-tipped.....22
22. Leaves in 2 rows, more or less in one plane.....23

22. Leaves in more than 2 rows.....31
23. Leaves with 2 prominent lateral veins from base of blade; lateral buds appressed; pith typically chambered ....*Celtis*
23. Leaves otherwise; pith continuous.....24
24. Leaves with main lateral veins dissipating into smaller veins before reaching the margin; fruit a small pome (apple-like); buds long and tapering ....*Amelanchier*
24. Main lateral veins extending into teeth of leaf margin; fruit not a pome.....25
25. Terminal bud long and tapering, at least 4 times as long as broad; leaves coarsely serrate; fruit a bur with two triangular nuts...*Fagus grandifolia*
25. Terminal buds less than 4 times as long as broad; leaves finely or doubly serrate.....26
26. Most leaves bilaterally symmetrical or nearly so.....27
26. Most leaves decidedly lop-sided, especially at base, leaf margins mostly doubly serrate ....*Ulmus*
27. Trunk and larger branches smooth, with fluted or projecting ridges, "muscular" in appearance; bud scales in 4 rows ....*Carpinus caroliniana*
27. Trunk without fluted or projecting ridges.....28
28. Some lateral veins forked; bark longitudinally shredded; lenticels inconspicuous; fruit completely enclosed in a papery sac ....*Ostrya virginiana*
28. Lateral veins unforked and continuous to leaf margin....29
29. Leaves evergreen...*Leucothoe fontanesiana*
29. Leaves deciduous.....30
30. Bark relatively smooth except in very old trees; lenticels conspicuous, laterally elongated on larger branches and trunk; fruit winged, in cone-like clusters ....*Betula*
30. Bark ridged or scaly; lenticels inconspicuous; fruit a samara ....*Ulmus*
31. Leaf-blades at least 4 times as long as broad.....32
31. Leaf-blades less than 4 times as long as broad.....33
32. Bud with 1 exposed scale...*Salix*
32. Bud with about 6 exposed scales.......................................*Prunus*

33. Buds distinctly stalked; fruit a woody cone-like structure ....*Alnus serrulata*

33. Buds not stalked; fruit otherwise.....34

34. Neither stipules nor stipular scars present....35

34. Stipules or stipular scars present....36

35. Leaves distinctly sour to taste, margins ciliate; twigs greenish-red...*Oxydendrum arboreum*

35. Leaves not sour; buds glabrous, covered with scales; flowers in clusters...*Halesia carolina*

36. Petioles with one or more glands near the blade; fruit a drupe ....*Prunus*

36. Petioles without glands.....37

37. Vein scar one...*Ilex montana*

37. Vein scars two or more.....38

38. Younger twigs averaging less than ⅛" in diameter; leaves finely and regularly serrate...*Amelanchier*

38. Younger twigs averaging more than ⅛" in diameter; leaves coarsely toothed or irregularly lobed.....39

39. Fruit apple-shaped ....*Malus*

39. Fruit pear-shaped ....*Pyrus communis*

SPECIES KEYS, ARRANGED ALPHABETICALLY BY GENUS

Acer

1. Leaves compound...*A. negundo*

1. Leaves simple.....2

2. Buds with 4-8 scales apparent, essentially sessile; flowers in lateral clusters; trees of various habitats.....4

2. Buds with 2 valvate scales, distinctly stalked; flowers in terminal racemes; small trees of mountains.....3

3. Twigs and buds glabrous; leaves finely serrate, with 3 main veins; bark striped with whitish lines.................................*A. pensylvanicum*

3. Twigs and buds pubescent; leaves coarsely serrate, with 5 main veins; bark not striped ....*A. spicatum*

4. Leaves usually with 7 prominent veins from petiole; leaf scars meeting; sap milky when evident; exotic trees frequent in city planting..A. *platanoides*

4. Leaves with 3 or 5 prominent veins from petiole; leaf scars usually not meeting; sap not milky; native trees.....5

5. Buds conical, exposed scales 6 or more..........................A. *saccharum*

5. Buds ovoid, usually 4 scales showing; flower buds rounded and collaterally multiple.....6

6. Lobes of leaves narrowed at the base; twigs ill-scented; bark flaking..A. *saccharinum*

6. Lobes of leaves not narrowed at the base; twigs not ill-scented; bark; tight, not flaking.....7

7. Leaves small, dominantly three-lobed..........A. *rubrum var. trilobum*

7. Leaves larger, dominantly five-lobed..............A. *rubrum var. rubrum*

Amelanchier

1. Leaves glabrous below; young leaves brownish-green..........A. *laevis*

1. Leaves pubescent below; young leaves whitish-green........A. *arborea*

Betula

1. Twigs with odor of wintergreen.....2

1. Twigs without odor of wintergreen..B. *nigra*

2. Bark on young trees and branches peeling, yellowish; cone bracts ciliate; leaves cuneate or slightly heart-shaped at base
....B. *alleghaniensis*

2. Bark on young trees and branches cherry-like, tight; cone bracts glabrous; leaves heart-shaped or rounded at base.............B. *lenta*

Carya

1. Buds with more than 6 overlapping scales; leaflets 3-9, the upper most largest......3

1. Buds with 4-6 scales in pairs, meeting at edges; leaflets 7-17, usually lanceolate, often curved......2

2. Leaflets 9-17, nut cylindric, longer than broad, shell thin, smooth; bark with flat, scaly, interlacing ridges........C. *illinoinensis*

2. Leaflets 7-13; nut somewhat flattened, about as broad as long, kernel bitter ....*C. cordiformis*

3. Larger terminal buds over ½" in length......4

3. Terminal buds smaller (less than ⅜").....5

4. Twigs red-brown to gray with age; leaflets typically 5, terminal leaflet stalked; bark splitting off in long strips ....*C. ovata*

4. Twigs bright brown to gray; leaflets typically 7-9, stellate-pubescent; terminal leaflet sessile or nearly so; bark tight...........*C. alba*

5. Leaflets typically 7..*C. pallida*

5. Leaflets typically 5.......6

6. Bark not becoming shaggy; leaflets 5, rarely 7; rachis and petiole green; terminal buds narrowly ovate-lanceolate, scales tight, not dotted, or if so, dots inconspicuous.................................*C. glabra*

6. Bark becoming shaggy; leaflets 7 or 5; rachis and petiole (sometimes only petiole base) red or red-tinged; terminal buds ovate, scale tips spreading, scales yellow-dotted.......*C. ovalis*

Celtis

1. Leaf blades seldom more than 2" in length; fruit dark orange-red, on stalks about as long as the petioles; small tree...........*C. tenuifolia*

1. Leaf blades usually more than 2" in length; fruit on stalks longer than the petioles; becoming large trees...........................*C. laevigata*

Crataegus

Several species of this difficult and confusing genus have been credited to Great Smoky Mountains National Park. Flower and fruit characters are required for identification. No key is attempted here.

Fraxinus

1. Leaflets not papillose beneath, margin often serrate; wing of samara often decurrent to middle of body or beyond...........*F. pennsylvania*

1. Leaflets papillose beneath, margin entire or nearly so; wing of samara terminal or only slightly decurrent along upper ⅓ of the body...*Fraxinus americana*

Juglans

1. Pith chocolate-colored; leaf scars with a downy cross-line at top, not notched; fruit longer than broad, hull sticky-glandular ....*J. cinerea*
1. Pith tan; leaf scars without a downy ridge at top, notched; fruit essentially spheroidal, hull not glandular..*J. nigra*

Magnolia

1. Leaves deciduous, not leathery.....2
1. Leaves evergreen, leathery ....M. *grandiflora*
   2. Leaves cordate at the base......4
   2. Leaves not cordate at the base.....3
3. Leaves 6-10" long..M. *acuminata*
3. Leaves 18-24" long..M. *tripetala*
   4. Leaves strongly auriculate, not whitened beneath, 10-16" long; petals 10-16" long..M. *fraseri*
   4. Leaves not strongly auriculate, pale to nearly white beneath, 20-30" long; petals 6" long ....M. *macrophylla*

Malus

1. Branches often armed with hard, sharp lateral spurs...M. *angustifolia*
1. Branches unarmed..M. *pumila*

Morus

1. Leaves rough above, more or less tomentose below, infrequently lobed; fruit red ....M. *rubra*
1. Leaves smooth on both sides, usually lobed; fruit white..M. *alba*

Picea

1. Leaves averaging ½" long..*P. rubens*
1. Leaves averaging ¾" long..*P. abies*

Pinus

1. Leaves characteristically 5 in a bundle..*P. strobus*
1. Leaves 2 or 3 in a bundle......2
   2. Leaves 8-18" long..*P. palustris*

2. Leaves much less than 8" long......3
3. Leaves characteristically 2 in a bundle; or in both 2s and 3s 4
3. Leaves characteristically 3 in a bundle ....*P. rigida*
4. Cones commonly asymmetrical, often more than 2½" in length, with very stout prickles..*P. pungens*
4. Cones usually symmetrical, with slender prickles, less than 2½" in length.....5
5. Branches nearly smooth; leaves twisted, usually less than 2" long, in 2s..*P. virginiana*
5. Branches scaly; leaves not twisted, usually 3 to 5" long, usually in both 2s and 3s ....*P. echinata*

Populus
1. Fastigiate (with upright branches)..*P. nigra*
1. Not fastigiate......2
2. Teeth small, more than 14 on each side........................*P. deltoides*
2. Teeth large, less than 14 on each side of the leaf blade.....3
3. Petioles averaging over 2" in length; twigs and leaves essentially glabrous..*P. grandidentata*
3. Petioles averaging less than 2"; twigs and leaves white tomentose ....*P. alba*

Prunus
(A difficult group when without fruit and flower characters)
1. Terminal bud typically present.....5
1. Terminal bud typically absent, represented by a scar......2
2. Buds elongate, longer than thick......4
2. Buds scarcely longer than thick......3
3. Leaves usually 2-4" long; calyx lobes glandular............*P. munsoniana*
3. Leaves mostly 1-2" long; calyx lobes without glands....*P. angustifolia*
4. Leaves thin, lustrous, acute or acuminate, crenate-dentate ....*P. hortulana*
4. Leaves dull, dark green, abruptly pointed at apex, sharply serrate ....*P. americana*
5. Twigs green or red..*P. persica*
5. Twigs reddish-brown or gray......6
6. Buds averaging 3/16" long; flowers in elongate clusters.....*P. serotina*

6. Buds ⅛" long or less; flowers not in elongate clusters.....7
7. Buds ⅛" long or less..*P. pensylvanica*
7. Buds 3⁄16 to ¼ " long (escaped, edible cherries).....8
8. Buds glossy, ovoid-fusiform...*P. avium*
8. Buds duller or darker, round-ovoid..................................*P. cerasus*

Quercus

1. Leaves characteristically entire (unlobed and untoothed) ....*Q. imbricaria*
1. Leaves characteristically lobed, toothed, or both......2
2. Leaves broadest near the tip (about ⅙-¼ length from the apex); not conspicuously lobed or toothed.........................*Q. marilandica*
2. Leaves broadest nearer the middle, with conspicuous teeth or lobes......3
3. Leaves with coarse teeth or scalloped but not distinctly lobed ....*Q. prinus*
3. Leaves distinctly lobed.....4
4. Lobes of leaves without bristle-tips......5
4. Lobes of leaves with bristle-tips.......6
5. Leaves glaucous and glabrous beneath at maturity................ *Q. alba*
5. Leaves densely gray-pubescent beneath............................. *Q. stellata*
6. Mature leaves more or less pubescent on the whole undersurface 7
6. Mature leaves smooth beneath except for tufts of hairs in the major vein-angles......8
7. Leaves brownish or rusty pubescent beneath, lobes not curved, frequently wider toward the end...*Q. velutina*
7. Leaves grayish or yellowish pubescent beneath, lobes generally curved and widest at the base...*Q. falcata*
8. Lateral lobes of leaves not decidedly longer than the width of the undivided portion of the blade; leaves dull, 7-11 lobed; acorn cup saucer-like..*Q. rubra*
8. Lateral lobes of leaves decidedly longer than the width of the undivided portion of the blade; leaves lustrous, 5-9 lobed ....*Q. coccinea*

Rhododendron

1. Leaves deciduous...*R. calendulaceum*
1. Leaves evergreen......2
   2. Leaf blades about 3.5 times as long as broad, tapering at base, green to brownish beneath..*R. maximum*
   2. Leaf blades about 2 times as long as broad, rounded at base, whitish beneath..*R. catawbiense*

Rhus

1. Leaf scars U-shaped; rachis winged.......*R. copallinum var. copallinum*
1. Leaf scars C-shaped or broadly crescent-shaped; rachis not winged 2
   2. Stems glabrous or nearly so; twigs often 3-sided...............*R. glabra*
   2. Stems hairy, concealing the lenticels; twigs rounded.........*R. hirta*

Salix

1. Branchlets strongly drooping..*S. babylonica*
1. Branchlets not strongly drooping.....2
   2. Leaves whitish beneath..*S. alba*
   2. Leaves green beneath..*S. nigra*

Ulmus

1. Leaves mostly less than 2¾" long; twigs usually with corky wings...*U. alata*
1. Leaves usually more than 2¾" long; twigs without corky wings.....2
   2. Bud scales coated with rusty hairs; leaves very rough above; pedicels short; fruit not ciliate; inner bark mucilaginous. ....*U. rubra*
   2. Bud scales without rusty hairs; leaves relatively smooth above; pedicels slender, drooping; fruit ciliate; inner bark not mucilaginous...*U. americana*

Viburnum

1. Outer flowers large, showy and sterile; drupes red.........*V. lantanoides*
1. Flowers all similar in size; drupes black or blue; leaves 3-lobed; palmately veined..*V. acerifolium*

GLOSSARY

ACHENE. Small, dry, seed-like fruit; does not open
ACUMINATE. Tapering to a slender point
ACUTE. Forming a sharp angle
AGGREGATE. Cluster
ALTERNATE. Not opposite to each other; leaves borne one at a node at regular intervals
APPRESSED. Pressed close to, or lying flat against
AURICULATE. With lobes or appendages at the base
AXILLARY. Relating to the axis or main stem
BILATERAL. Relating to two corresponding sides
BIPINNATE. Doubly or twice pinnate
BLADE. The expanded part of a leaf petal, or sepal
BRACT. A specialized leaf
BRANCHLET. The final or farthest divisions of a branch
CALYX. The outer, usually green or leafy part of a flower, contrasted with the inner showy portion (corolla)
CAPSULE. A dry fruit usually containing two or more seeds
CILIATE. With marginal hairs
COLLATERAL. Side by side
COMPOUND. Blade divided into leaflets
CONTINUOUS PITH. Pith not interrupted by hollow spaces
CORDATE. Heart-shaped
COROLLA. The petals of a flower, collectively
CRENATE. Margins scalloped
CRENULATE. Margins finely scalloped
CUNEATE. Wedge-shaped
DECIDUOUS. Not persistent; falling off at maturity
DECOMPOUND. More than once compound
DECURRENT. To extend downward
DENTATE. Toothed; the teeth directed outward
DIAPHRAGMED PITH. Pith is interrupted by papery partitions
DRUPE. A fleshy fruit with a hard inner portion
ENTIRE. Without teeth or divisions
EVERGREEN. Not deciduous
FASTIGIATE. Erect and close together
FOLIACEOUS. Leaf-like
FUSIFORM. Spindle-shaped; tapering at each end

GLABROUS. Smooth; lacking pubescence (hairs)
GLAND. A secreting organ
GLANDULAR. Containing or bearing glands
GLAUCOUS. Having the surface covered with a grayish, powdery bloom or coating
HERBACEOUS. Having the characters of a plant that has no persistent woody stem above ground
HUSK. The outer covering of various seeds or fruits
INFLORESCENCE. The flowering part of a plant
INTERNODE. The portion of a stem between two nodes
LANCEOLATE. Lance-shaped; broadest toward the base
LEAFLET. One of the divisions of a compound leaf
LEGUME. Fruit (pod) of the Fabaceae
LENTICEL. A small corky spot or dot on young bark
LOBED. A deeply divided leaf
MEMBRANOUS. Thin; soft; pliable
MUCILAGINOUS. Becoming slimy when chewed
NODE. Place on a stem which ordinarily bears a leaf or leaves
OBTUSE. Blunt
OPPOSITE. Leaves borne two at a node on opposite sides of the stem
OVATE. Egg-shaped; broadest near the base
PALMATE. Leaflets radiate from the end of the petiole
PANICLE. A compound raceme
PAPILLOSE. Rough with minute blunt projections
PENDANT. Hanging down
PERSISTENT. Remaining long attached
PETIOLE. A leaf stalk
PINNA. One of the principal divisions of a pinnate or compoundly pinnate leaf
PINNATE. Leaves arranged in two rows along the rachis
PITH. The spongy center of a stem
POME. Fruit resembling an apple
PUBESCENT. Bearing hairs on the surface
PULVINUS. An enlargement of the petiole at the point of attachment to the stem
PUNCTATE. Dotted with minute spots
RACEME. A type of inflorescence in which the elongated axis bears flowers on short stems, the lowest opening first

RACHIS. The continuation of the leaf stem as the axis of a pinnately compound leaf
RENIFORM. Kidney-shaped
SAMARA. A dry winged fruit, usually one-seeded
SCURFY. Covered with small scales
SERRATE. Having sharp teeth pointing forward
SERRULATE. Finely serrate
SESSILE. Without a stalk
SIMPLE. A form in which the blade is not divided into leaflets
SINUATE. Having a wavy margin
SINUS. The space between two lobes
SPHEROIDAL. Almost a sphere
SPINOSE. Spine-like
SPUR BRANCH. A short branchlet
STELLATE. Star-shaped
STIPULE. One of a pair of small appendages borne near the base of the leaf stalk (if petiole)
TOMENTOSE. Wooly; covered with densely matted hairs
TRIFOLIOLATE. Having three leaflets
TRIPINNATE. Thrice pinnate
TRUNCATE. Having the end square, as if cut off
UMBELLATE. An inflorescene in which flowers radiate from a single point
UNDULATE. Wavy margins
VALVATE. Meeting only along the margins; not overlapping

INDEX

NOTES

INCHES

1 2 3 4 5